Let Them Manage

A SMALL BUSINESS GUIDE TO PEOPLE MANAGEMENT

ROBERT STELL FCCA

CONTENTS

About Bradbury Stell Payroll and Personnel Ltd

Bradbury Stell Payroll and Personnel Ltd is a part of the Bradbury Stell Group which also includes the following:

- **Bradbury Stell Chartered Certified Accountants**
- **Rise Audit**
- **Bradbury Stell Probate Services**

Bradbury Stell Payroll and Personnel Ltd principally runs payroll services for clients that need it, enabling them to keep a confidential digital file for each employee. This file would contain a P45/P60 along with a signed Employment Contract, sickness and holiday records. It would also contain a signed staff handbook.

FOREWORD

The HR industry has, in my opinion, received a great deal of unfair criticism for its role within commercial life. My view is that the HR function should never be used as a substitute for real management. Real Managers should hire, fire, develop and appraise their own staff. These are the fundamental pillars of the business of management. These roles should never be delegated to the HR function, for in doing so Managers will dilute their own vision and message.

As the Chief Executive Officer of your own company, this book is for you, whether you are in a position of hiring your first member of staff or you already have a team under you. The development of this team is your responsibility. There is no HR Department... **you are the HR Department!**

The easier parts of the HR process, such as keeping records and payroll, can and should be outsourced very cost effectively. For a smaller business, my contention is that the more challenging side of the HR process should be managed by you. It is your responsibility to develop, hire and dismiss (if necessary) **your** staff. Principally this book is a guide for you, the owner, to better manage your people.

There are skills and technical knowledge that you must learn first. This book is designed to help you with both. It is both a concise summary and useful handbook in an increasingly complex HR landscape, ignorance of the law is sadly no excuse and it could cost you dearly.

This book contains reference to current HR law and the relevant documentation as it stands in the UK right now. The book also contains

useful tips and strategies for managing your people. Your people are your greatest asset, manage them correctly and you will achieve great things.

Enough of the waffle, let's get started!!

HIRING AND INTERVIEWING SKILLS

Your business will expand and rapidly prosper if you ensure that the people you hire are cleverer than you. Always remember that the key resource in your business is the people within it and if you employ really good people, your business will definitely prosper.

If you are hiring to replace someone who has left or is soon to be leaving then chances are that you already know what job that person's subsequent replacement is going to be doing.

Let's imagine for a second that you are hiring someone into a job that doesn't yet exist. When I say it doesn't yet exist, I mean that you are probably doing some of those tasks yourself and you want to delegate those to someone else in order that you may free up your time to do the things that you are best at. Spending time doing things you are not good at is a waste of time and it will limit your progress. Almost certainly there are tasks that you are less than average at – so be honest with yourself about this and delegate them as soon as possible. If you don't let go... you won't grow!

The first task is to draw up a job description. The job description is a detailed list of all the tasks that this person would be expected to perform. Along with this is a brief 'wish list' of tasks that you would like this person to carry out in the future. As an example; you, as the CEO of your own organisation, are currently doing the payroll, the credit control, paying your suppliers and at the weekends.... trying to reconcile your bank account. You start on Monday morning feeling exhausted and you have little time, enthusiasm or energy to do the thing that you are really best at, which is naturally business development. The thing that seems to be taking all your time is credit control and you are doubtful whether you are the right person to do this because it often means finding the time to talk directly to your client, which can of course be awkward.

So, primarily you want someone to come in to take over the credit control function, but it would also be nice if they could do payroll, and wouldn't it be great if they could have experience of doing the bank reconciliation too? The probability is that if they can do the former two tasks, you can train them into doing the third.

"I want that employee motivation study by Friday or you're sacked."

So what qualifications would/should this person have? They would definitely need to have credit control experience, as this task is one that requires a degree of tact, diplomacy and patience. They may be training to be an accountant, they may just be a part time bookkeeper, they could be a range of different kinds of people. After you have decided upon a job description, you must also then decide how much time you would require this individual for each day/week/month. The next thing you have to decide is how much you are willing to pay them and under what conditions? Are you going to provide flexible working, or are you going to require them to work fixed hours? Will you subsidise their travel into the office? Might they require a car allowance?

As you will no doubt see throughout this book, I am a big fan of flexible working. Being able to offer flexible working conditions will certainly mean you are going to have a broader selection of people to choose from and subsequently a greater rate of retention.

How much should you pay them? The answer to that, from your point of view, is as little as possible! Remember, all of this money is coming directly out of your pocket and you are going to feel very loath to part with any of it. The problem, however, is that if you don't pay enough you won't get the right person. This particular bullet has to be bitten.

How do you find out how much is the right amount? LinkedIn is a source of this kind of information as is Mr Google generally but Recruitment Consultants are the best source.

Even though your business is small, I would still recommend using a Recruiter at this point. First of all they are the experts in remuneration

"Welcome aboard, Withers. Now just go see Personnel on seven, and Pants on Twelve."

for the kind of job that you are looking to fill and they will save you an awful lot of time (if they are any good) in shortlisting people for interview.

They are/can be expensive, and you will be charged anything between 15% and 20% of the starting salary (plus VAT!) for the privilege of finding someone that you might have found anyway. The problem here is time.

Yes, if you had enough time, you would likely find this individual yourself. You could put up the advert on LinkedIn and you could trawl through all the responses and eventually pick out a shortlist for an interview but, as we have already established, time is a precious resource that you don't have.

So how do you get started?

The first task if you are going to use a firm of Recruiters is to recruit your Recruiter. Recruitment firms tend to specialise in a particular sector, e.g. Accountancy, Marketing, IT Consultancy etc etc. A quick search of Google will bring up a list of Recruiters in your area. You will need to meet these Recruiters and ideally they should come to your office or place of business. There is no point in going to theirs! They have to be at your office or place of employment to understand the culture and to understand where this new employee will be situated. If they are unwilling to visit you then they have failed at the first hurdle.

Once you have met your Recruiter, you'll need to be on the lookout to see if they ask all the right questions about your business (they need to be asking you lots and lots of questions about you, your business, your plans, your aspirations etc). You are looking for someone who is bright, inquisitive, motivated and, having asked you lots of questions, also understands your business and your requirements. I would suggest you use between two and three Recruiters but definitely no less than two. Whilst they would prefer sole custody of resourcing for the vacancy, you must resist this! There is very little upside for you to just use one Recruiter. Recruiters do not charge until a successful placement is made so all of the work that they will be doing to resource and shortlist suitable candidates is effectively work done without charge.

How do you find out how much is the right amount to pay?

The best resource for finding out remuneration rates for specific roles are with the agencies that specialise in recruiting for those roles. For accountancy, the major agencies are Reed and Hays. Ordinarily they will provide this information free of charge and particularly if you are meeting them to use their services.

So, let's say you have decided on two Recruiters. You have given them the job description and they have told you what the appropriate salary is. The next stage is the bit that they are supposed to be better at than you, and that is drawing up a shortlist. I suggest you get each Recruiter to draw up a shortlist of no fewer than five people. You will also need to see all of their CVs.

You will need to specify to the Recruiter the minimum level of experience that you are looking for and the minimum qualifications. If either of the Recruiters sends through information of a candidate that does not meet these minimum specifications, my suggestion is that you dismiss that Recruiter and get another. I know that sounds a bit harsh but if they can't follow simple instructions (which many of them can't) you should move on.

From the Recruiter's shortlist of five candidates, you should narrow that down to three for a telephone or Teams/Zoom interview. This interview does not have to be very long at all. It is not a substitute for a face-to-face interview, merely a prequalification. If someone cannot express themselves clearly over the phone, then it is highly unlikely they will be able to express themselves clearly face to face.

You would start the telephone interview by saying "Hello, thank you very much for calling me. This is just a very very quick chat of no more than a couple of minutes ahead of a potential face to face interview". Then, you would ask an open ended question that affords the candidate an opportunity to talk directly to you. A suggested open-ended question is "So, what interests you about this job?". After that you must let them speak. As they are speaking you will form some idea about their lucidity, qualifications, experience, confidence etc, perhaps even making some brief notes to reference later. The telephone interview really is about 'ruling out' unsuitable candidates instead of an evaluation process of their suitability. The evaluation process starts at the first interview. This is all about whittling down the shortlist.

After the telephone interviews are complete, hopefully you will be left with four or five candidates that you would like to see face to face. Let's say that two came from one particular Recruiter and three from the other. Once you have made your shortlist you should act quickly in arranging their appointment bearing in mind that they will be looking at other opportunities as well.

The recruitment process should be pretty sharp at this point. My personal preference for interviews is first interview one week, and a second interview either at the end of the same week or at the beginning of the next. There are many reasons why I like to separate them out. Firstly, it gives the candidate plenty of opportunity to think of any questions that they may have missed between the first and the second interview (and the better candidates will definitely have questions). Secondly, it gives me time to think about each candidate a bit more deeply and to think of any questions that I might like to ask them on the second interview.

The second interview stage should also involve at least one other person. This could be a fellow employee, a spouse, or even an external professional. You will need someone else's point of view. Whilst that person's role does not include asking any technical questions, their opinion on the candidates' personality, fit and character will be extremely useful when it comes to making a final decision.

Let's return to the first interview stage. You would hope that the candidate would arrive on time and be dressed appropriately. 'Appropriate dress' could be anything that is suitable for the task.

A very useful acronym to remember for attending the first interview is WASP which stands for Welcome, Acquire, Supply and Part.

W is for **welcoming** the candidate into your office or to your premises and it is very important to get this right. Your welcome needs to be friendly, open and direct, thereby setting the overall tone for the rest of the meeting. It is a welcome in the same way that you would welcome a sales prospect. What I like to do at my own business is to welcome them in, get them settled in the office and then leave them while I go downstairs and make them a drink of their choice and make one for myself. I don't rush this task because it allows the person to familiarise themselves with their surroundings and to calm down a bit. Remember, they will have made a journey to meet you. Your office could be in an area that is unfamiliar to them so when they arrive they will be nervous and unrelaxed. Leaving them to relax a little will make them feel more comfortable which is, after all, what you want them to be.

A is for **acquire**, which is one of the most important parts of the interview process. This is about you acquiring knowledge about them. Ideally you will already have prepared a list of questions from their CV on topics such as: where they grew up, what their school was like, what their favourite subjects were, their last job, what they liked about their last job, what they didn't like, their aspirations for the future, what they think they are good at, etc etc. You want the candidate to talk about themselves. You will want to hear about their achievements but you will also hopefully want to hear that they are confident but modest about those achievements. You may also find that this is an excellent way to identify any discrepancies between their lived experience and what was included in their CV. After all, writing certain embellishments is much easier than being able to articulate them.

S is for **supply**. Once you have acquired all of this information about the candidate, you will be in a position to supply them with information about your company, your own aspirations, the role in the company that they are being interviewed for, what you expect from them, what further training they might get and how they might develop within your company. Once you have done all that talking, you would probably ask "do you have any questions at this point?".

Those that are not interested in your company and the job will merely want to know how much they are going to get paid, how much they get for lunch hour, what the holiday entitlement is etc. My recommendation for candidates like that is that they are not to be considered for the second interview stage.

You are looking for someone who has listened to what you have said and wants a little bit more depth about certain aspects of the role or the development possibilities within the role. Perhaps they desire a little bit more information about how your business works, how it could be more successful and how they could help in driving future growth. In other words, you are looking for someone who is already thinking themselves into the role. Once these questions have been answered, that is effectively the end of the first interview.

P stands for **part** as in parting. This is the last bit that the candidate will remember, so it must be positive and must leave the candidate with the impression that they are still in with a chance. You should mention that they will be contacted by the Recruiter and if they are selected for a second interview, that interview would be held by the end of the following week. This should give the potential candidate time to make the necessary arrangements so that they are available at the time you want the second interviews to be held. Thank them for their time, see them to the door, shake their hand, smile etc.

So from the five first interviews you will need to remove the weaker candidates from the shortlist so that you are left with a maximum of three for the second interview stage. You know that these people speak well on the phone, have the right qualifications, can speak to you face to face in a confident and bright manner, are well motivated and they are all keen to take on this role.

For the second interview, you will once again welcome them in exactly the same way, comment on how good it is to see them again, find out about how their week has gone, settle them down as before, get them a drink etc etc. Once all of those pleasantries are out of the way the first question you would ask of them is whether they had any questions as a result of the first interview. I think of it as a good sign if they do have immediate questions. It's highly unlikely that they would have understood and grasped everything that you had said at the first interview and what you would hope is that they would have been thinking about the role in the week since the first interview and those thoughts would have prompted some questions.

After they have asked those questions and you have had a conversation to explain the answers, it is time to ask them any questions that you have as a result of your thought process in the week since the first interview. At this point you will bring in your second and maybe even third interviewer. You will leave the room having briefed the second interviewer about what you want them to talk about. In my view, unless the second interviewer is an existing employee that has the necessary technical experience to ask detailed questions, they should really be very general open- ended questions, where the candidate is given a chance to talk openly.

When that stage is over, you will then wrap up with the candidate and again ask them if they have any further questions they would like to ask. At this point I like to ask them whether they would take the role if offered. Now you may think it would be a given fact that the candidate would still be keen to take the role, but sometimes that is actually not the case. It could be that through the second interview process they have started to become uncertain, so they may say that they need to give it some thought, or something very similar. In my view, that is a signal that they have doubts. If they are at all hesitant at this stage, my suggestion is that you rule them out. When the interview is over and you part company you inform them that the results of the interview process will be available in a few days. A few days is the absolute maximum.

I prefer to have all of the second interviews done on the same day so that you can make the decision at the end of that day. You will again need to be quick in making your decision and making contact with an offer or decline because if these candidates are any good, they are going to be having interviews with other potential employers.

At this point, you need to talk to the people that have been 'pressganged' by you into doing the other part of the second interview and ask their opinions. I like to wait until I have interviewed all the second interview candidates before I ask the second interviewer what their opinions are. These opinions are quite often very interesting and sometimes quite different from the opinions that I had already formed. Hopefully you and the second interviewer will agree on who the best candidate is and at that point you need to inform the Recruitment Consultant so that they can break the happy news (and sad news to those who have missed out) as soon as possible.

The agent will hopefully then have those conversations with the candidates and get back to you with feedback very quickly. In all of the cases where recruitment has gone wrong for me, there has been a delay between me imparting the news to the Recruiter and the Recruiter confirming the news that the candidate wants to take the job. Where there is a delay it almost certainly indicates that the candidate is not wholly enthusiastic. This could be because they are deciding between a number of jobs or it could mean that they have some doubt about the role that you are offering them. Either way, this delay will almost certainly lead to problems later on. I cannot offer you a definitive solution to this problem but I can say that if the delay is significant and the second candidate was a close second, you might want to choose the second candidate in any event. I know this sounds like a bit of a bold and risky move but I feel that someone coming into your organisation who is anything less than red hot keen, is not the one for you.

Hopefully you will receive the happy news quickly that the candidate has accepted your offer and in that event you need to get an offer letter to them as soon as possible by both email or Royal Mail. The offer letter should have the following information in it:

- When they should start
- A starting salary
- Hours of work
- Holidays per year
- Study days per year (if applicable)

See over page for example of offer letter.

Example of offer letter:

Ref
Date

Mr/Mrs/Miss XXXX XXXX
House Number
Street Name
Town
Postcode

Dear XXXX

It is with great pleasure that I can confirm your appointment as JOB TITLE with COMPANY NAME to commence on _____

Your salary will be £XX,000 per annum pro rata based on X days per week (XX hours). If you successfully complete your three month's probation, you will become eligible for our study package. The study package will be:

- XX days study leave with up to £X,000 expenses per annum paid in respect of this.

- Your holiday entitlement will be XX days per annum plus Bank Holidays.

I very much look forward to seeing you on _____ and most office staff start between X and X.XX am.

Kind regards
Yours sincerely

REMUNERATION AND REWARD

Below are the outcomes that employees **really** seek from their employment:

- The need for autonomy
- The desire to do the right thing
- The aspiration to be connected to something bigger than themselves
- The drive to do work that feels significant and meaningful

But... employees also need to be rewarded 'correctly'.

The important aspect to financial reward is to take the 'issue' of money off the table altogether i.e. to make sure that money is not something that your employees think about.

An interesting facet of human behaviour is that the biggest issue for employees isn't how much they get rewarded but whether they feel it is fair in relation to how much others have been rewarded. Our response to pay and rewards is not absolute but comparative. The problem with reward is that high rewards don't necessarily motivate, but low rewards will definitely demotivate. The important thing to remember about 'reward' is that it is not just remuneration. Human beings will react to praise and recognition in the same way as they react to remuneration.

Studies have shown that praise and recognition ignite the same areas of the brain as financial reward. In just the same way as giving too great a financial reward has less and less marginal utility, the same is also true of praise and recognition.

There is an art to praise and recognition, and that is:

- Only give it where it is due
- Do not overuse it
- Use it at the point of delivery, not weeks and months later

It is very rare that any bonus system will improve performance, or rather improve **individual** performance. It's much better that if you are going to have a bonus system to make sure that the bonuses are linked to overall team performance instead of performance by individuals.

So what is a 'low' salary? A low reward is a salary that is below the market level. If someone is paid below the market average, they will likely think ill of their employer, inasmuch as they will think that their employer is taking advantage of them. It's not necessarily that they want more money for its material use, it's just that they do not want to be treated with disrespect. One of the key things about reward is that you should always know where the market level is and make sure your employees are paid at least at that level.

DELEGATION AND EMPLOYEE DEVELOPMENT

When you started your company, You...Did...Everything. As time went by, however, you realised that you needed other people within the business to lighten the load, so that you could continue to expand the business. That process continues year after year as you share more and more of the tasks that you had previously performed. When you set up your business, you will have realised that there are a small number of things that you do extremely well, a large number of things that you are not particularly good at, and probably a few things that you are completely hopeless at! So it makes sense therefore to start with the latter group when it comes to delegation. If you are lucky and you hire the right people, you will end up in a business where you only do things that you are very good at and enjoy.

"I'm afraid you don't have the leadership qualities we're seeking."

Over the years I've come to realise that in reality, delegation and employee development aren't actually two separate topics because at the point of delegation you are actually developing that employee's skillset.

The first thing to mention about delegation is that delegation is not abdication. Once a task is delegated to a member of your team, it is not the end of the story. There will always need to be a follow up on that delegation. After you have successfully briefed a relevant member of the team on both what the task is and how they should go about it, you need to let them know that you will be checking in with them in the next few days (or weeks) to find out how they are getting on. It should go without saying that you need to make it very clear to them that they should come to you at any time if they feel that they are struggling with that task.

What is an appropriate follow up action?

Firstly, there needs to be two-way communication from that person to you as to how they should go about that task. Should they have any problems with it, they need to be able to have access to you to find out how to remedy any problems they are experiencing. Also, you need to check in with them, certainly in the early days, to make sure that they have grasped what it is that you require of them and you should give them honest feedback as to how they are doing with that task.

A prospering business will require giving your people delegated responsibility, that is **real** responsibility, and it also means that you must allow them to make decisions that are independent from **you**. You must ask yourself "do I want a successful business, or do I always want to be right?"

In my own business I believe that one to one communication with new customers is a task that I perform better than anyone else in the company. This is not something I would wish to delegate because I do believe that it is one of the small number of things that I am extremely good at. Why would I wish to delegate that job to anyone else in the company? If a client has a problem with any of the work that our firm has done, then at some point I have to step in and try to resolve that situation. The client would not accept me delegating this to someone else. This role is something that I can see myself doing for a very long time, and the company would have to be extremely large for me to delegate that responsibility. Taking personal responsibility for your company is something that you, as the owner, must always try and do.

"This really is an innovative approach, but I'm afraid we can't consider it. It's never been done before."

Delegating a task should not be a long list of detailed steps as to how the task is done. Maybe that would be appropriate for a brand-new employee but as time goes on, you should take out more of these steps so that in the end, you are in fact only giving a broad framework of how you would like the task to be completed. This enables the employee (given that they have had sufficient training) to think more for themselves about the best way forward to completing the task. If you have made that framework too vague or too loose, they should come and tell you. Your team will relish the opportunity to think for themselves and use their own initiative. The good ones will always rise to this challenge. One of the paradoxes of leadership is that by delegating and giving away power, you develop other people. This doesn't in fact make you look weaker, it makes you look stronger.

Now, the problem with delegation is that you have to teach someone else how to do the task which takes time and of course you have the risk that they could mess it up and you may have to do the clearing up afterwards, but you **have** to allow your people to fail because if they don't, they won't grow as individuals and it means that your company won't grow. As long as there is an open and honest channel of communication between you and your staff, failure will be seen as a learning event and not as a disaster.

When passing on a task to someone else, it's always a good idea to ask that person to explain it back to you. You might see them nodding as you explain the task but they might just be doing that because they want to appear to have understood and avoid looking stupid. If they can explain it back to you but they have got it wrong, be kind, be patient and re-explain it until they do understand. The worst thing you can do is to develop a situation where your employees are so scared of you, they will always say that they have understood what you have told them to do, but in fact they haven't understood at all. If your communication style is open, honest and friendly they will have no problem asking for clarification of what it is that you are asking of them.

If, after a while, it appears that the task has been successfully delegated and taken on by the individual, don't forget to acknowledge their efforts. Thank-yous and acknowledgements in my view should be used sparingly – because they are **that** important. If used sparingly, they will hold more value than if you are telling people that everything is awesome all of the time.

When delegating it is easy to assume that the person you are delegating to is going to be enthusiastic about taking on this task. You need to remember that some people are fearful of making mistakes and others aren't bothered if they do. Those that aren't bothered about making mistakes are in a group of people that need to be eased out of your company as soon as you can. Those that are fearful are those that have respect and that fear should be treated gently. The individual must be encouraged slowly so that they gain confidence and can take on more tasks. There is no greater feeling than making those fearful types more and more confident over time! The overly confident individuals who bite off more than they can chew and don't understand all of the detail, thus underestimating the task, can be very dangerous indeed.

STAFF REVIEWS

It may come as a bit of a shock to you but once someone comes to work for you, it's not just a job. You are now responsible for a part of their career development. They will want to know from you what their objectives are over the coming months and more specifically how achieving those objectives will also help your firm achieve its objectives. Staff reviews, therefore, are extremely important.

The staff member whose career you are now responsible for will also want to know what you think of them. You might just think that once you have given them the job to do, they can just get on with it and that's the end of that. But, you must remember how you felt when you were an employee and the thought of "what does my Boss really think of me" was very often on your mind.

I strongly suggest that the first review for your new employee should be after about three months and this should be quite informal. What I mean by that is that it shouldn't be a written review, it should be just a chat. The first three months of any employment are the most stressful as the new employee is not only getting used to the task at hand but also the office environment and the people they are working with.

The most important thing about this chat is that you ask them how they are feeling about the work and the people they work with. You should understand whether they feel they are being adequately supported, adequately remunerated and adequately trained. Discussion will often flow from there, because you are talking about their requirements rather than talking about **your own**. This initial interview is by its very nature all about them. You will learn from this chat who they get on with, who they don't get on with, what they think of the work, whether they find aspects of it difficult and how they see the rest of the year unfolding.

From your perspective you must reiterate what you want from them, as this would have been discussed at the initial interview some time ago. Hopefully they will be enthusiastic and you can also take the opportunity to paint a broader picture of how the company is doing and how important it is that their efforts are feeding into the overall performance of the company. It is human nature to want to be a part of a team and to have your efforts in that team respected and acknowledged. So hopefully at the end of that meeting the employee will feel motivated and reassured as to their place in your company.

"We like you, Hatcher, and we like your work, but we've been offered magic beans."

From there on, the reviews of staff performance should be, in my view, at least twice a year. The annual review should be in depth, with the mid-year review being a catch-up. Of course, there is nothing stopping an employee coming to chat to you if they want clarity and reassurance at any time of the year. This should, in fact, be encouraged.

"Your performance review is next Tuesday. You're allowed to bring a guitar and up to three backup singers."

Although your employees will be operating within their own bubble, they also want to hear what things are like from your view as the owner and CEO. Of course they want to know that it's mainly good news but I think that it's best to share the good with the bad and to be (more than anything) realistic. What I tend to do once a year with my staff is to produce a two-page broadcast catch-up. On the first page is a review of all the things that I wanted to do in the last year, hoped to do in the last year and maybe didn't do in the last year. It's a chance to recognise things that were achieved but which weren't necessarily planned. It is a time for bold honesty as regards any mistakes that were made and celebrate successes, whether big or small.

The basic facts of the company's turnover rise and fall and profit rise and fall should also be revealed at this juncture. On the next page of the review I always outline a schedule of my plans for the company over the next twelve months. Again, detail is important as the employees like to know what it is that you are planning to do. The plans, as ever, must be realistic and achievable because if they are not then come twelve months hence you are going to have to tell your staff why you failed to achieve your goals. It's a time for honesty and self-reflection but your staff will like you for trying and they will appreciate your honesty.

One of the benefits of this exercise is not only the benefit of self-reflection but it also helps the employees think about how their efforts, their job description and their objectives fit into the overall company objectives. This is known as 'goal congruence', i.e. where the employees' personal objectives align with the company objectives.

The next part of the review process which I think is very key is a questionnaire to the employee. Again, just like in the interview stage and the first review stage, this forms the basis of the discussion which you will have with them at their review. Below is a version of a questionnaire that I have given my own staff.

Staff Review Example:

Please let me have the following information:

- Your current salary
- When you started at the firm
- Your starting salary
- The number of hours you do per week and your FTE days holiday per annum
- How you feel your career has developed in 2023 (exams, experience etc). Please be as detailed as possible ...... including where you think you did particularly well compared to the previous year
- What was 2023 like for you - workwise and in your personal life? Be as honest as you dare to!
- What jobs in the rotation you are yet to do
- Your views of what changes the firm should make in 2024
- Your views on my plans for 2024 and beyond. Be honest......if they are confusing or unclear or even if you don't agree with them, tell me

Their answers to these questions will reveal an awful lot about what they think of the company, their future, the company's future and how ambitious, (or not), they are. Once you have had your answers back from them, you are in a position to give your review of their performance back to them. Then you are ready to have your chat.

You may think that this is a rather longwinded process and perhaps wonder "what is the point"? The reason is that this meeting should have no surprises in it. It should be serious and be a document to refer back to in the months to come, particularly in one year when the next review comes around.

If there was anything deficient in their performance you should have raised that long before the review, unless by some chance they have caused a problem just recently.

It must also be said that employees do not respect performance reviews that are glib and insincere. "Everything is awesome all of the time" is not what employees want to hear. They want to hear constructive, detailed advice about how you can help them achieve their goals. It could be technical, or it could be personal or it could be about their communication style. If you point out to an employee that there is a certain area that needs to be improved, you must also point out how you are going to help them to make that improvement. As I said above, when you are approaching their performance review, you should be talking about fine tuning their performance rather than wholesale changes. Those 'big' conversations should have been had during the year, if at all. My view is that if you had an employee on board who needed wholesale changes then they are probably not the right fit and you should be referring to the chapter on dismissal. I know that sounds harsh but it is harsh for a reason and fair for all concerned.

I give below an example of a performance review. It is brief and written in a friendly and conversational style. It is meant to be motivational and hopefully send that employee forward with a sense of purpose for the year ahead.

Bradbury Stell Staff Review 2023

Connor Smith

2032 production target £120,000, production achieved £133,000. An extremely large number, which exceeds the number I referred to as a would be 'magnificent achievement' a year ago.....so there is not much else I can say!!

So yes, I agree with you, a very good year indeed.

The role of operations manager is to 'get the work in, get the work done, get the work out' (as measured by billing). In which case, since you took on this role, you have done extremely well. It clearly suits you.

In 2023 you started out into leadership and this will become a much bigger part of your future, not just here but wherever you go to afterwards. I think that the chat you initiated about Andrew was a demonstration of leadership. You saw the damage being done and saw that I wasn't aware of it. It was an important intervention. I think I have now steered Andrew into a clearer, narrower path, but he still may be a problem. It is a situation that requires careful monitoring.

Jack and I have talked a lot about production quality. We both think that the 'buddy' review system, although expedient, may lead to a dilution in quality. As operations manager, this isn't really your concern per se, but Jack will be exerting more control in future over production quality. Ironically this (theoretically) could lead to tension with you as you seek to hit the billing budget.....but actually I am sure it won't and anyway I think that tension would be a good thing. We don't want to veer too much towards quantity at all costs, or towards quality at all costs. There has to be a balance. In future I will be shown the review sheets and will be stressing to staff that I want to see five or fewer review points. More than ten will be seen as a real problem.

I would like you to compile that list of roles and responsibilities, particularly whilst I go through the hiring process for a new admin person. I think it is only important for Alex, Ravi and Andrew and I suggest you start this by asking them what they perceive their responsibilities to be. That way you can see if there is any overlap/gap.

Software and hardware are being improved as we speak. Harry is buying new PC's and Jack is installing a replacement to PTP and new payroll software.

I agree about the layout of the office. I do not think we have the budget to complete this in 2024, but we can make a start. Andrew is going to arrange for the disposal of the cabinets and we will look into getting more desks like the one you sit at. Maybe another two this year. There is no excuse for all the other clutter and just like with the sink.....it is up to personal responsibility OR for the seniors (Jack, you and Harry) to instigate a clear out. Clutter is de-motivating.

Your production target may seem steep, but remember fees have gone up.

Your salary will rise to £40,000 from £36,000

2024/25 Target production £80,000.

Robert Stell March 2024

Performance Appraisals

Always remember that the performance appraisal is a two-way process. It's not just about you judging the abilities of another human being, it's about them judging you and the organisation that you lead. It's a two-way conversation. By putting the word 'appraisal' into the title of the conversation, are you not perhaps creating something that is potentially confrontational? My suggestion is to leave the word 'performance' out of it because that is perceived as a judgemental word and instead just call it an annual review because it is, and should be seen, as an opportunity to review all aspects of the company, of the individual, of you as a leader, of the leadership structure and the company prospects etc.

The obvious problem with ambushing an individual with bad news is that their defence mechanisms will naturally kick in. The result? A meaningful dialogue is unlikely to take place. All that will in fact happen is that you start to create fertile ground for an argument. An argument during an annual review is the last result that you want.

Be open to listening to their view about you as well. I do not recommend asking direct questions such as "what do you think of me?" but leading with more constructive questions such as "where do you think the company could improve over the next year" or "where do you think the department could change its procedures" or "what changes in IT would make doing your job easier" would be useful. These are the questions that get employees involved in trying to make changes to your organisation and their own job satisfaction. I heartily recommend that you avoid any kind of grading or rating system when appraising your employees. The idea behind the review is a two-way conversation. Subjective views expressed in a 'rating' can drive down people's enthusiasm and particularly confidence or even worse, make them think that they are better than they really are.

Staff Training

Staff development should also include external training. I once worked at a global telecommunications company and they had a policy that everyone had to take five days of external training every year. There was a 'menu' of the different types of training you could undertake, some of which was internal and some of it was external. Clearly, this company had invested a great deal in training and they also had incredible staff retention rates to prove its success. In my view this is no coincidence. For a small company, providing five days of external training a year is likely to cost several thousands of pounds per employee so it should be considered carefully. But staff really do have a very high regard for ongoing development opportunities. It shows that you are taking their career seriously and that you are prepared to invest in that person.

You should have an honest chat about the kind of training that they feel would be beneficial and compare it to the sort of training that you feel they should have. There is no point trying to train a person in something they have no interest in. I give as an example a member of staff whose communication skills are quite poor. Unless they admit that their skills in this area are lacking (and some people just never

ever see it) it is highly unlikely that you are ever going to be able to get them to commit to any training to improve this area.

Training doesn't have to be based outside of the office. A trainer can be brought into the company's premises and the training could even be done online (either as a group or one to one online). Clearly the most expensive kind of training is where an individual travels to the external training session. Those kinds of training sessions are, I believe, the best because it takes the employee out of feeling like they are still at their place of work. It means, in my view, that they are more likely to have a clear mind and therefore more open to receiving new ideas.

If you also run an accountancy firm, most of your training budget will be spent training your staff to pass exams that qualify them as an accountant. This is similarly true in many other professional firms but what if your staff are not training for a professional qualification? Is training really still important?

It is absolutely important. It is important on many levels. It is not just that the member of staff sees that you are investing something in them but obviously you are hoping training will improve their performance at work. It may not be performance in a narrow technical sense, but it could be performance in a broader sense e.g. becoming a better supervisor, manager or having better communication skills etc.

I don't think training, however, should ever be seen as a fix. For example, "let's send this person on a course because they are not very good at talking to other people" because I think that the message the employee receives is, "Oh I'm not very good, I need to be sent to school to get better". I think all of your staff need to be given some latitude as to what it is they want to be trained in.

ADMINISTERING A PAYROLL

Once you have employed your first member of staff, you will have to administer a payroll for them. This is absolutely not something that you should do manually and my strong recommendation is that you outsource this immediately, as it is a technical and increasingly complex task.

"That £20 deduction is for new benefits – like the £10 raise you just got."

Understandably it is expensive to use an outsourced payroll provider. As an example, my firm Bradbury Stell Payroll & Personnel Ltd would charge around £400 per year (at the time of writing) for a single employee. The tasks that you must perform for that employee in terms of the payroll are as follows:

- Processing the monthly payroll and ensuring that the right tax and National Insurance is deducted.
- Producing a payslip and delivering it either by email, physically or via a portal.
- Filing the RTI (Real Time Information) monthly through the HMRC website.
- Paying over to HMRC by the 19th of the following month the PAYE and NI that you have deducted from that employee.
- Providing the employee with an annual P60 statement of their earnings.
- Filing the annual statement to HMRC.
- Issuing P45s as and when necessary.
- Administering SSP (Statutory Sick Pay).
- SMP (Statutory Maternity Pay)
- Deducting and administering the company's pension scheme.
- Ensuring the employee is on the correct tax code
- Calculating holiday allowance

As you can see from the above it's quite a long list of responsibilities and very painful if you get it wrong.

Statutory Sick Pay (SSP) and the Law around Employee Sickness

Your employees will be ill, that is just a fact of life. Not often, hopefully, but they will. My own view on employees' sickness is that although you, as a self-employed person, are probably not ill very often, other mere mortals are! In other words, it's best not to have a derisory view about other people's physical wellbeing. Yes indeed, they may be 'throwing a sickie' but that's not the biggest crime in the world as long as it doesn't happen very often of course.

The law around sick pay is actually very confusing. As an employer you are not obliged to pay a member of staff who is off sick UNLESS they have been off sick for four days or more and can provide medical evidence of their sickness. In this case, they will be eligible for statutory sick pay (SSP) which is payable at the rate of £99.35 per week at the time of writing up to a maximum of 28 weeks. There is no legal obligation to pay anybody anything at all if they are off sick for just three days. This does seem a little cruel and I think if you were to follow these strict legal parameters, you won't be winning 'Employer of the Year' anytime soon. If it is only a day or two, you may well be better off just paying them as if they had come to work.

Your actual policy on sickness should be clearly stated in the Contract of Employment. An example of a Contract of Employment is outlined in Appendix I. If the nature of your business and the nature of the work is such that you really cannot afford to cover their pay if they are ill, you must clearly state that in the Contract of Employment.

If your employee is consistently taking time off ill, the chances are that the illness is a manifestation of their disinterest in working for you. A frank and honest conversation with that employee is almost certainly the best way forward if that is the case. In my experience the conversation will either lead to the employee divulging their dissatisfaction or unease working for you or shortly thereafter you will get a resignation.

Jury Service

The law around paying employees during jury service is quite similar to SSP. You are not legally obliged to pay an employee who has been selected for jury service as they will be able to claim compensation directly from the Court. You may want to carry on paying them as normal or you may indeed top up their Court allowance to make sure that they are not in any way out of pocket from their public duty.

Statutory Maternity Pay (SMP) and Paternity Leave

Statutory Maternity Pay is now common within major developed countries and is a fantastic way of keeping key staff engaged in your organisation for the long term. The key thing to remember is that the maternity pay is effectively paid for by the Government. The practical reality is that you, the Employer, have to pay it but you claim that against your other PAYE and National Insurance obligations.

The basic mechanics of Statutory Maternity Pay are as follows:

- It is payable for up to 39 weeks and can start before the birth or just after. The pay period is not quite the same as the leave period, in that an employee has the right to take up to 52 weeks although only 39 of those will be paid.

- Your employee will need to produce to you a MAT B1 Certificate issued by their GP which will indicate the expected due date of the child. Your employee can choose the start date of the SMP and statutory maternity leave. Some like to work as long as possible, some like to take more time off before the birth if they are actually ill at any time in the last four weeks before their baby's due date, then the SMP kicks in at that point automatically.

- The employee will get 90% of their average weekly earnings before tax for the first 6 weeks and then £156.66 or 90% of their average weekly earnings whichever is lower for the next 33 weeks.

- All female employees will qualify for Statutory Maternity Leave but not all will qualify for Statutory Maternity Pay. In order to quality for SMP an employee must earn on average at least £123 per week, have given the correct notice and given proof that they are pregnant and have worked for you continuously for at least 26 weeks.

There is still a feeling that persists amongst employers that the words 'statutory maternity pay' or indeed 'pregnancy' are a threat to the company. In my experience, the opposite is true. An individual returning from maternity leave is much more likely to be loyal and hardworking provided you, as the employer, can offer sufficient flexibility around their childcare arrangements.

Pensions

One of the most onerous duties for employers that has come along in the last ten years is the administration of pensions for employees. The rules regarding the administration of pension schemes as recently introduced by the Government (known as auto-enrolment) are as follows:

An employer must automatically enrol an employee into a pension scheme and make contributions to their pension if they are eligible for automatic enrolment. If the employer does not have to enrol the employee by law, the employee can still join their pension scheme if they want to. The employer cannot refuse.

However, the employer does not have to contribute if earnings are these amounts or less:

- £520 a month
- £120 a week
- £480 over 4 weeks

When enrolled into a pension scheme, employers must:

- Pay at least the minimum contributions to the pension scheme on time – usually by 22nd of each month.

- Let employees leave the pension scheme (called 'opting out') if they ask – and refund money they've paid if they opt out within one month.

- Let the employee re-join the scheme at least once a year if they have opted out.

- Enrol the employee back in at least every three years if they have opted out and are still eligible for automatic enrolment.

Holidays

Employees who work a five-day week must receive at least twenty-eight days paid annual leave a year. This, however, does include all Bank Holidays which number, on average, eight in total.

DISMISSAL, REDUNDANCY AND OTHER EXITS

If you are the owner of a business and you employ people, one day you will be responsible for dismissing someone. Never a pleasant task, but a necessary one. Not just for you, your business and your team but also for the individual who has found themselves in the wrong place at the wrong time. In many cases, it can be a great kindness to let them go, allowing them to move on to find something better suited to them.

First, let's go through the legal aspects of dismissing an employee.

You must set out your dismissal and disciplinary rules and procedures in writing. If you do not, a tribunal can order you to pay an 'employee compensation'. Your dismissal and disciplinary rules should be written in the Contract of Employment.

Dismissal is the term used to describe when an employer ends a contract of employment – and they do not always have to give notice.

If an employee is dismissed, employers must show they have:

- a valid reason that they can justify
- acted reasonably in the circumstances

They must also:

- be consistent - for example, not dismissing an employee for doing something that they let other staff do
- have investigated the situation fully before dismissing someone - for example, if a complaint was made about a staff member

A part-time or fixed-term worker cannot be treated less favourably than a full-time or permanent employee.

Acting reasonably

Even if you have a fair reason, the dismissal is only considered fair if you also act reasonably during the dismissal and disciplinary process. There is no legal definition of 'reasonableness', but if you are taken to an employment or industrial tribunal they would consider whether you:

- genuinely believed that the reason was fair
- carried out proper investigations where appropriate
- followed your stated procedures
- told the employee why they were being considered for dismissal and listened to their views
- allowed the employee to be accompanied at any disciplinary/dismissal hearings
- gave the employee the chance to appeal

If you are alert to the performance of your team, will become quite obvious if any employee is not fitting in. It could be that their personality doesn't fit into the culture of your organisation or it could be that their technical competence is not what you need it to be. Either way, if your systems, procedures and workplace culture are as you would want them to be, the one that doesn't fit should stand out pretty quickly.

All employees starting a new job will make mistakes. It is a sign of a healthy culture that mistakes are allowed to be made without fear of any fingers being pointed. People learn quicker by making mistakes than if they were to learn from a handbook. Once the mistake has been identified, it should be pointed out to the individual swiftly so that they can learn and move on. This should be done verbally and in a helpful tone, not one where the employee feels that they are being reprimanded.

The problems tend to occur when the employee makes the same mistake over and over again. In this instance it becomes clear the employee either does not have the capacity to learn from their mistakes, (which could be a technical deficiency), or they are not sufficiently interested in the role or the technical aspects, to rise to the challenge. This might be despite your giving them all the sufficient resources. It may just become clear over time that the employee is in the wrong job. At this point a written warning needs to be issued. A written warning via email is perfectly sufficient, and in my view is the ideal medium.

The written warning should be in the form of a reprimand, because it is a follow up from a previous verbal warning, but it should also be helpful. After all, the individual needs guidance on where they should improve, how they might do so, and when you will be following up.

Here is an example of a first written warning:

Dear Anthony

Previously, we have spoken about the need to improve the quality and accuracy of your work. Unfortunately, we have not seen adequate progress since our last conversation and wish to provide additional support to improve your performance henceforth. I have a tip for you which always helped me when I first started - always wait at least twenty-four hours before sending your work for review.

Do the work, put it to one side and do something else. By the time you pick it up again it will look like you are looking at someone else's work. When you finish something, it is hard to spot the errors, that's why you need to leave it a bit and then come back to it.

You will improve, don't worry, just don't rush so much.

The aim of the written warning is not to terrify this member of staff, they will be as embarrassed as you about the error that they have made. What they are looking for from you as the leader is some methodology for improvement. It's no good just to say to someone "that's wrong, do it better". You have got to be able to suggest a way that they might get better.

Now let's assume, unfortunately, that the first written warning has had no effect. It could be that the employee does not have the technical capacity to rise to this challenge even though you have given them all the sufficient resources. It could be that the employee is not that interested in the role and doesn't want to spend time learning how to do this better. If it is the latter, the employee is likely to leave before you even issue the second written warning.

The second written warning is where you now state that this has become a very serious matter and they must think very hard as to whether they want this job or not, because there isn't going to be another chance for them to remedy matters. In my view, the space between the first written warning and the second written warning should be a decent period of time, perhaps at least a few weeks, because you need to give people time and space to try and resolve their faults.

Here is an example of a final written warning:

> Dear Anthony
>
> I am sure you will understand that a business such as ours cannot survive if employees make repeated errors. I know that you are capable of getting this right but I do need you to start getting it right quite soon. We have spoken verbally and have also had a first written warning exactly four weeks ago.
>
> I am afraid that this is the last time you will be warned about your performance. Any further errors such as the one I attach in this email will sadly lead to your dismissal. If you feel that you are not being instructed properly by either myself or your immediate supervisor or you feel that you do not have the resources available to make further progress, do talk to me urgently. This is a serious matter and we do need to make progress here and move on, one way or the other.

The tone of the second letter is considerably darker than the first. In my view, it is because by the time you get to the second written warning you are in fact close to the end. You do need to give the employee the chance to remedy it but in my experience it is highly unlikely that anyone comes back from a second written warning. In fact what normally happens is that once the employee has received the second written warning, they will take some time to reflect and quite often they come to the conclusion that this isn't the job for them, and their resignation letter or email arrives several days later.

I believe that this outcome is, in fact, the best way out for all concerned because it does at least mean that the employee is taking matters into their own hands rather than having their future decided for them. Of course, the only thing to do if you do get their letter of resignation is to offer them your best wishes and reassure them that you will help them as much as you possibly can to secure further employment.

Where I can, I will always send on details of agency contacts that I have who could help them either in securing new employment or in determining what their next best career move is.

But let's just imagine that the employee does not resign, stays put and sadly does not improve their performance. Clearly the axe must fall, to use a rather dramatic phrase, but that phrase does at least sum up the speed and finality of the decision that you must make. It is not fair on your team to have an under-performer bringing everybody's tempo and morale down.

Everybody has a different view as to how the final act should be played out. There are some that prefer the traditional "can you come into my office" where you will be sitting accompanied by a member of HR to witness the event and to hold the axe! Everything is read out to the employee and they are told to leave the building immediately and hand in all their passwords, keys etc.

Personally, I feel that method too cold and can become quite a shocking experience for the employee. Their adrenalin is likely to rise extremely sharply which will almost certainly mean that their thinking won't be clear. They may get aggressive, they may get tearful. Either way it is all a fairly unpleasant experience. It might seem controversial, but I think that it is easier to send an email to the employee asking them not to come into the office the next day or in fact not to come into the office until asked to do so. Tell the employee very honestly that you will be having some internal discussions and meetings about their performance and they will be informed within the next few days as to what next steps should be taken.

What this does is take the heat out of the moment. The employee will be angry and distressed, but at least they can internalise that when they receive the email instructing them to stay at home. I have done this on a number of occasions, and on all the occasions that it has happened, the employee has handed in their notice within forty-eight hours. It still leaves the employee thinking that they have taken the action, rather than you. It is much better for an employee's self-esteem to believe that they left their job rather than that they were sacked from their job.

Clearly, if you do not get that resignation email, you must inform the employee, within the forty-eight-hour period that you promised, that their employment is at an end. You can offer them a chance to talk to you about it face to face, and if they like they can also bring someone else to that meeting. They are indeed owed that, but in my experience this will never happen. If you do wish to meet them face to face, I do strongly suggest that that meeting takes place off-site in a neutral environment. You really don't want your team to witness the cast out member of the tribe returning.

If you are dismissing them, it is best to give them salary in lieu of them working their notice. In other words, if their contract notice period is one month, you will pay them one month's salary plus any outstanding holiday pay at the point of dismissal. This does have the effect of cushioning the blow at least financially.

Redundancy

"I'm not sure what I was doing, but, evidently there's no call for it anymore."

There is a huge difference between the dismissal of an employee and redundancy of an employee. This large legal difference means that there are different financial implications for both outcomes. The key aspect of a redundancy is that it is not the person that becomes redundant, it is the position that they hold. So in other words, redundancies happen when positions are closed down permanently. Now that the position has been closed down, the person occupying that position is no longer required (on the assumption that they cannot be absorbed into another part of the business). When someone is dismissed on the grounds of poor performance, it is likely that the position they held will remain open for future candidates.

The legal aspects to redundancy are as follows:

Employees you make redundant might be entitled to redundancy pay - 'statutory redundancy payment'.

To be eligible, an individual must:

- be an employee working under a contract of employment
- have at least two years' continuous service
- have been dismissed, laid off or put on short-time working - those who opted for early retirement do not qualify

The statutory redundancy notice periods are:

- at least one week's notice if employed between one month and two years
- one week's notice for each year if employed between two and twelve years
- twelve weeks' notice if employed for twelve years or more

You must make the redundancy payment when you dismiss the employee, or soon after and the first £30,000 of that payment is free of tax.

A redundant employee also has the right to a written statement setting out the amount of redundancy payment and how that has been calculated.

In my opinion making someone redundant is far worse than dismissing someone. When you make the decision to dismiss someone, as difficult as it is, the rest of the team normally breathe a sigh of relief as it means there is an opportunity for someone better to come along and they don't have to continue carrying that 'passenger'. When there is a redundancy, however, the team will sense that your business is failing. Why would the boss be laying people off and making them redundant if the business wasn't contracting? This scenario therefore has the potential to spread fear throughout the team and this potential for fear has to be managed very carefully.

It could be that the redundancy is in fact because that particular process can now be automated and human hands, therefore, are no longer required. If the person that is in that position cannot be redeployed elsewhere (they may lack the skills to do so), then redundancies are inevitable and in fact, to do so can be seen as progressive because your organisation is embracing new processes and technology.

But, what if you are making someone redundant because of economic contraction? As in all other forms of dismissal, you need to act quickly, fairly and humanely. For you to have come to the decision that redundancies are inevitable, you must have made a forecast into the future and decided that business is about to decline, and that there are people in your team you are no longer going to need.

But, what if you are wrong? What if you lay off a couple of people now and in fact the economy doesn't turn down but picks up again in six to nine months? What a shame to have paid out all of those redundancy payments to people who are familiar with your processes and are both popular with the team and with customers! What a pity to lose all that! My preference, instead of redundancy, is to have a phased approach, or at least to offer a phased approach. Rather than laying off one person, why not try asking five people if they would be prepared to reduce their pay and hours by 20%? In my experience, particularly if the team is large enough, one in three people will probably accept that. This largely has something to do with the way the tax and National Insurance is deducted, so a 20% reduction in gross pay quite often does not lead to anything like a 20% reduction in net pay, plus people get an extra day off. This may well be a better way of keeping the team together so that you can quickly take advantage of the upturn when it comes.

Also... consider an alternative to redundancy. This following example was a tactic employed by a major company in the US after the 2008 financial crisis. In return for no redundancies across the whole company, the company asked all employees to take twenty-eight days unpaid leave. This did not have to be consecutive days, it could be taken at any time over the next twelve months meaning that the 'pain' could be spread. One thing that happened immediately was that the employees no longer feared losing their livelihoods. They also no longer feared imminent lack of income. The policy gave the employees time to plan ahead for the next year and to take the unpaid leave at a time convenient to them. For instance, they might consider tacking it on the end of planned paid leave. When the recession was over, the workforce was still intact and was then able to take advantage of the upturn in the economy. The renewed 'esprit de corps' within the workforce meant that their overall performance was higher than before the financial crisis.

Of course, getting employees to alter the terms of their contract will need the buy-in from all employees. If a significant number of the employees don't agree to this, then that could present a problem. This is a case where your persuasive skills as the leader of this organisation really come into their own.

Other Exits and What They Can Tell You

It is always sad when an employee leaves your organisation, particularly when they are a valued employee. If you have done everything you can to keep them and that means the following:

- told them of their worth
- paid them the right amount of money
- given them every opportunity to develop their career in your company

and they still look for opportunities elsewhere, all that means is that they are ambitious people. Do you want ambitious people working for you or not?! Chances are that you have both benefitted from the working relationship and that employee should now fly the nest and spread their wings. There is always value, however, in talking to that person about their experiences in your company, their opinion of how you run that company and if there are any opportunities that you are not taking. It is worth asking the following four questions of them;

- what are the good things that your company does?
- what are the bad things that your company needs to stop?
- what are the things that your company does occasionally which they should do more of?
- what are the things that your company doesn't do at all that they should do?

The key question is, of course, when you should be doing this interview..... if at all. If you have that interview any time before they actually leave your doors, they will give answers that they think you want to hear. In other words, potentially untruthful ones. In my view, the value of the exit interview is at the three months post leaving stage. They will be in their new organisation, they will be familiarising themselves with their new company and they will be in a good position to compare that organisation with your organisation. If you can, I suggest getting their views through someone else e.g. another team member. Clearly this is not always attainable, but they are more likely to give the truth to someone else than they are to you. What they have to say may well not be entirely to your liking but you have to remember that there is huge value in the views of departing employees.

It is, of course, a good idea to keep in touch with your old employees and if you have staff get-togethers, don't forget to invite former employees to them. You never know, one day they may come back!

COMPANY POLICIES AND PROCEDURES

Health and Safety

Most employees these days work in an office where there is very little need for concern around health and safety. I don't in any way wish to demean the risks involved in working in an office but it's not exactly like working in a coal mine or a cotton mill in the nineteenth century. There are still dangerous places to work, of course, building sites for example are still responsible for a hundred or so deaths in the United Kingdom every year.

There is a basic requirement for all employers to provide a Health and Safety Manual. This may be long or may be short but it needs to cover some very basic contingency planning and should cover the following topics:

Provision of adequate lighting, heating, ventilation, adequate workspace, toilets, washing facilities and refreshments, safe passageways, i.e. by preventing slipping and tripping hazards.

As with any kind of manual, the longer it is the less likely it is that it will be read. If you regard the manual as being of importance to the staff, then make sure it is written in a way that will encourage people to read it. Just like this book contains cartoons to visually engage the reader and to make a connection between what is being written and what is seen, why not do the same with your Health and Safety Manual? Fifty pages of do's, don'ts, must do's etc etc etc are almost certainly going to be completely ignored. If you are working in an environment that contains hazards, it is important that your staff understand what the health and safety rules are. If there is any possibility of something bad happening, one day it will happen, and the more employees you have, the greater the risk of that 'something bad happening' – so plan for it and make sure people know what to do when it happens.

Contracts of Employment

The issuing of a Contract of Employment to a new employee is now a legal requirement. Contrary to what you might think, a Contract of Employment does not necessarily have to be a long, legally complicated document. As with any document it should be written clearly and should be as brief as possible.

See Appendix I at the back of this book for an example of a Contract of Employment and the key points about it.

Sack the HR Department?

Policies and procedures make the HR Department feel better but they are often at best ineffectual and at worst damaging for the employees' morale. Quite often you don't need more rules and procedures, you just need to let your staff act and behave like the adults they are. One thing there is absolutely quite enough of is 'rules' and there are not enough rules in the whole world to keep everyone completely safe.

Why not just have one policy? 'Employees shall not do anything that will not be in the interests of this company'.

Why not just leave it at that?

Why not just treat your employees as adults and not children? Do they really need any more than that? Clearly, they do and the procedures and policies should be further detailed, but I tend to bear this in mind; treat your employees as adults who can think for themselves, and are not criminals. The reality is that when we trust our employees and they see that we trust them they are more productive, more creative, more loyal, and more responsible. It is therefore also true that the more rules you put in front of people, the more likely it is that those rules are going to be disobeyed, skirted around or completely ignored.

One of the key problems with policies and procedures is that they are often centred on threats, rather than rewards. We all know that when staff are given increased levels of autonomy, they are more likely to be creative and will solve problems on their own and they will think laterally. The problem is, of course, that we don't trust them! And at its worst this is what the HR function is about. The HR function can be the department that stops people from thinking for themselves.

An effective HR system should motivate staff rather than threaten them. Staff are motivated by three things. Firstly, autonomy. Secondly, when they are given the opportunity to master the tasks that they like to do. And thirdly, they are working at a company that has meaning. In other words, they feel connected to something bigger than themselves.

Before writing any policy or procedure, ask yourself this question first of all – "**does** this rule exist because we don't trust some of our people to do things properly?" If the answer is yes, then obviously the conclusion must be that you are a distrustful person and your words are likely to come over as patronising! As an extreme example, do you need a policy that says 'stealing from the organisation will be met with instant dismissal?'. This is so obvious it doesn't really need stating either.

An area that is often thought ripe for abuse is reimbursement of employee expenses. Interestingly the company Netflix has a policy that is just 'always act in the best interests of the company'. Personally, I think that something as open ended as that could also be interpreted in a million different ways. I think that if you were to employ such a policy you would eventually find that some people would abuse it. You would therefore need to police it carefully and point out those abuses, but how could you ensure that they were at all times consistent?

The reality behind employee expenses is that an employee should not pay for anything out of their own pocket whilst they are carrying out their duties on behalf of the company. This is most often evident when someone has to travel away from their home on company business. You wouldn't expect them to sleep in a car but you also wouldn't expect them to stay in a five-star hotel. You would hope that they would act reasonably and choose a hotel of moderate cost. If the cost was immoderate, but there were reasons behind that, you would hope that the employee would explain it. Of course, we wouldn't want employees to waste time getting prior authorisation for something that maybe they had had to organise in a hurry.

Similarly, if an employee is flying to a location to save time, you would not expect them to be flying first class. Likewise, we would not expect them to drive the whole way there and back as this would waste time and energy and doesn't further the cause of the company one bit. However, we would leave that to the employees to decide. They don't have to eat their evening meals at McDonalds every night but then again, we wouldn't expect them to eat at a Michelin starred restaurant either. We expect the employees to take the quickest route to the assignment, stay somewhere that is going to give them a comfortable night's sleep and eat somewhere that is going to give them a nutritious meal. It's obvious really when it's laid out like that, and any employee who decides to push the boundaries will soon stand out and it is at that point that their motives must be questioned.

A second thing to be considered when writing any policies and procedures is that they need to be designed to allow your staff to think for themselves. For example, do you need a policy telling staff that they shouldn't be using social media during work hours? If those work hours are partly from home how on earth would you police that even if you did have such a policy? Treat your employees like adults! If they want to go on social media all day, let them go on social media all day. They know what their objectives are, let them work out how to get the job done.

Thirdly, if you get yourself into a situation where you have to refer to the guidelines in order to work out what to do next, then I suggest that you are in a difficult place. If you have to look at the policies and procedures to decide whether something is right or wrong then you have not conveyed what it is that your company is trying to do. It should be obvious.

Finally, always write your rules and policies from a position of trust, from a position where you expect employees to think for themselves and act in the company's best interests. Ask yourself whether you need a policies and procedures manual at all. Why not just set out general guidelines and principles?

"Well, that's it then, the motion is passed. Honesty, as a policy is out."

HOW TO BE AN EFFECTIVE LEADER

Gallup – How to Measure Employee Engagement

There are twelve needs managers can meet to improve employees' productivity. This approach to engagement is simple, and it works. These are the twelve employee needs that make up the items on Gallup's engagement survey:

1   I know what is expected of me at work.

2   I have the materials and equipment I need to do my work right.

3   At work, I have the opportunity to do what I do best every day.

4   In the last seven days, I have received recognition or praise for doing good work.

5   My supervisor, or someone at work, seems to care about me as a person.

6   There is someone at work who encourages my development.

7   At work, my opinions seem to count.

8   The mission or purpose of my company makes me feel my job is important.

9   My associates or fellow employees are committed to doing quality work.

10 I have a good friend at work.

11 In the last six months, someone at work has talked to me about my progress.

12 This last year, I have had opportunities at work to learn and grow.

"What kind of a mission statement is that?"

You are the leader of your own company. Those underneath you will expect you to lead in a rational and calm way. I can't emphasise enough how important it is to be calm. As Rudyard Kipling once famously said in 'IF', "If you can keep your head while all around you are losing theirs ….." Remember that you can only control your own emotions, you cannot control the emotions of others. If one of your employees loses the plot, it is imperative that your emotions remain unaffected and always remember that silence is the best way of calming any situation. Employees always respect a calm boss.

Communicating to your team about what you are doing and where you are going is important. However, I am not a great believer in meetings for meetings sake. I think staff meetings should be held no more than once a month and they should be short, sharp and succinct. No more than forty-five minutes with an agenda prepared beforehand. I think opening the staff meeting is key but, again, whatever you say should be short and to the point. You should have this loosely prepared, i.e. bullet points thoughts that you want to make prepared in your head so that when you come to speak, they will come out without the Ums and the Ahs. Don't overwhelm your team with lots and lots of detail. I think no more than four points should be made at any given staff meeting. The more you say, the more chance that people will forget it. Although they are all sitting around nodding their heads, only sixty percent of what you have said will actually have gone in. It is purely a reflection on how much humans understand when spoken to.

Just like in the Staff Reviews, the section of the staff meeting that is you speaking to them should all be along the same lines, which is:

- Where are we going?
- How are we going to get there as a team?
- How can you contribute to that effort individually?
- How long is it going to take?

Don't be afraid of repetition. Even though you see a lot of nodding heads, the reality is that you are going to have to repeat the message again maybe one month later and maybe again the month after that. This doesn't mean that your people are stupid, it's just normal human behaviour and repetition does not in fact annoy people, it just makes your message clearer.

There is a difference between positivity and 'boosterism'. The latter is a form of expression which would indicate that everything is **awesome all of the time**. People soon get tired of this. So in my opinion, you should be realistic but you should also be on the positive side of realism. If you are not on the positive side of realism then why on earth do you have a business? Realistic and positive goals that are achievable by you and your team will increase your team's self-belief. Unrealistic goals set by you for your team, that are not achievable due to their unrealistic nature, will destroy **your** authenticity and credibility.

Things will go wrong. This is an inevitable fact. As sure as night follows day, things will go wrong. If it has gone wrong and it's your fault, own up to your team. If you own up to your own mistakes it will encourage them to own up to their own mistakes. The boss owning up to mistakes is incredibly important and emboldens your team to take on challenges without fear.

Listening

Listening is something that most people find difficult to do. It is often thought that the stereotypical leader is someone who only transmits and never receives. Effective leadership, however, is the other way around. When a member of your team is talking to you, keep still, engage them fully in the eyes and say nothing until they have finished. Don't at any point give the impression that you want the other party to get on with what they are saying more quickly. If you are still and silent they will get their point across in their own time.

When speaking, use open questions such as; Who, What, When, Where and How. Beware of using the word Why as it can, if used incorrectly, imply criticism. As much as possible, reflect back to the speaker what your understanding is. This will have the effect of confirming to them that you are listening and understanding. As an example, when the negative employee outlines a problem ask them "what do you think we should do about this?".

Multi-tasking and Time Management

Studies have shown that the human brain cannot perform two cognitive tasks at the same time. Whilst it is possible to talk and cook, it is not possible to write an email and reconcile a spreadsheet at the same time or write a presentation whilst holding a telephone call. The cognitive process in the human brain is a linear processor. Multi-tasking is a myth. Effective time management means, as much as possible, concentrating on one task at a time. Do not be tempted to believe you are superhuman just because you're the boss!

Authenticity

As a leader you must be consistent. If you are someone who seems to change their mind all the time, you will lose credibility. It may sound obvious but under-promising and over-delivering will improve your credibility and authenticity over time. Over-promising and under-delivering will destroy it in no time.

If you are consistent with your own visions and how you go about things, your people will start to be able to predict how you will react. Your visions and your principles should be the same as the company's visions and principles which in turn should be the same as the team's visions and principles. I see no harm whatsoever in having these written down.

Decision Making

Making any decision that is going to affect your team requires thought. In my view, quick decision makers are always people who will gain more respect from their team than prevaricators. Provided, of course, that those decisions are always consistent within a broader framework of objectives, are fair and are followed through.

Before making decisions, try to seek the opinions from senior members of your team, and prepare to have your views challenged! If the senior members of your team feel that they can talk to you very directly, and their views would be heard and considered (even if they are rejected), then you will retain respect. Always, always sleep on any big decision. Don't take any rash decisions on the spur of the moment. Leave it at least twenty-four hours before you make your final judgement. Quite often, after a night's sleep, the solution will come to you while you are having your morning tea/morning shower as the brain does an awful lot of processing overnight that you are not conscious of.

Don't over-analyse is my advice. Paralysis by analysis will do you no favours at all and will make you look weak and indecisive. Bear in mind that decisions you take are never going to be perfect but if the upsides outweigh the downsides, then you must act. Not taking any decisions because of the possibility of downsides means that no decisions will ever be taken at any time. It's all a risk, but as long as you balance that risk you will come out ahead more times than not.

As ever, don't underestimate the value of your partner's view (I'm talking here about your domestic partner rather than business partner). Even if that individual has no background or expertise in your business, their view is valid. Sometimes the best decisions can come out of their honest and open questioning. Bear in mind that they have a vested interest in you getting it right.

MANAGING EMPLOYEE BEHAVIOUR

Flexible Working

If your business is manufacturing, only some employees will ever be able to work from home. However, the world economy is moving increasingly away from manual labour such that many of the tasks that are now performed are done so through a computer.

The location of the computer can be in the office, it can be at home, could even be a laptop on a beach – the point is that it literally could be anywhere. What we've learnt as a nation, as a result of the Coronavirus pandemic, is that forced working from home was not the productive nightmare that we thought it was going to be. In many cases productivity actually rose. Staff, who we perhaps assumed couldn't wait to lounge on the sofa and watch Netflix all day, are people that can be trusted to perform without you constantly watching them.

So, how is this apparent paradox so easily attained?

In my world of accountancy, the tasks that my staff have to perform are ones that are, generally speaking, best performed in silence. Concentration is important, and the tasks we deal with are complex. On the other hand, staff need to be able to talk to their colleagues about the solutions to client problems. If they are working from home, they can't do that. But if they are working in a busy noisy office, their concentration will inevitably suffer.

What I have found in my own company, is that the best solution is a hybrid mix of working from home and working in the office. Human beings are social creatures and they need to be with other human beings, so it is important that people do come into the office, but it is also important that they are offered flexible working times. An employee may wish to do three half days and one full day per week in the office and the rest from home, as an example. As an employer, bearing in mind that you wish to avoid a deserted office, it is better to leave it to them to work it out. If you treat people like grownups, surprise surprise they behave like grownups!

Considering the cost of travel and of feeding oneself away from home, switching from full time in the office to part time in the office gives an employee an immediate and substantial pay rise. Not only that, but they also won't have to waste two to three hours a day getting into work, time which is better spent working on your business.

How fresh and ready do you think the average employee is after having had to stand on a train nose to nose with a complete stranger for an hour and a half? Flexible working times means that rush hours can be avoided at the beginning and even at the end of the day. This will definitely lead to a fresher and more motivated employee.

What I have found is that when employees do want to come into the office, they quite often look forward to it as it now becomes the minority of their seven day week.

There are, of course, as ever, some legal aspects to consider when offering employees the opportunity to work from home. These are:

- Home workers are still entitled to sick pay.

- In fact, apart from the change in their place of work, the terms and conditions of their employment contract will, in the vast majority of cases, remain the same.

- Employers have a duty of care to ensure employees are not working more than 48 hours a week on average unless the employee has specifically opted out of the 'working time directive'. With the switch to home working, there is a possibility some employees will find it hard to 'switch off'. Though very difficult to track accurately, try to look out for signs of over-working like the time of day employees are sending out emails etc.

- Employers are responsible for data security even if the data is kept at a worker's home. Basic checks should be done to ensure staff are suitable as home workers.

At the beginning of 2020, not many of us had heard of Zoom or Microsoft Teams. Their use is now commonplace within most companies. But, what some people have started to suggest is that these types of meetings are far more exhausting than face to face meetings. The science behind this will develop over time but what is initially apparent is that the brain has to work much harder in a Zoom meeting than it does in a face to face meeting. Partially this is because you are looking at yourself for some of the time in a Zoom meeting, which of course you would never do in a face to face meeting! Also, because you can only see someone's head and shoulders, there is a lot of body language that you cannot see. We know from interpersonal contact that body language does give an indication of many responses, for example, agreement... or doubt.

Working from home does mean that your team must take more responsibility between them for making sure that some members are physically available in the office. No client likes to be told that the person they are looking for is not in the office today. A good telephone system will enable calls to be sent through to mobile phones as well as other extensions so that a client calling in doesn't necessarily have to know that your member of staff is not physically in the office. My opinion is therefore to treat the people who are working from home as if they were in the office as far as clients are concerned and to make sure that customers' needs can be met wherever that person physically is.

Dealing with the Disruptives

The disruptive member of staff can come in many different forms and as an example, there is the 'always present' type who constantly wants to be seen to be asking questions. They think that this will make them look inquisitive and engaged in your business. The interesting aspect to this behaviour for me is that they seem to put all of their energy into asking the question and when you explain the answer to them, their interest seems to fade. As far as they are concerned, they have achieved their objective in asking the question in the first place. They are not the type of person who wants to gain knowledge, they are people who purely want to make a point to you, their boss. These are also the people that in meetings will say "shouldn't we be doing this?", "shouldn't we be doing that?" as some kind of general statement of general non-specific policy for you and the company to consider. This makes them appear intelligent and broad in their thinking. But they only ever ask the questions and they rarely if ever offer the strategy or solution.

So how should you deal with these people? In my opinion... ruthlessly.

The reason being is that they will sap your time and energy. It could be that the individual is genuinely curious and of course genuine curiosity is something to be admired and developed. They may also want specific answers to specific questions in order to perform their role. Both of these are admirable but when that person appears to be asking the same questions over and over again and even after six months does not appear to have picked up even the basics of your business, you have to conclude that that person is not listening and their agenda is not aligned to your own. A close eye needs to be kept on these types and if the behaviour persists, you must look for ways of either getting them to change their conduct or get them out of the company.

The problem with disrupters is that they can appear to be the brightest person in the room. Sitting next to them may be someone who hardly ever talks but crucially gets the job done quietly and efficiently. Don't make the mistake of promoting the disrupter over the quiet one, as the disrupter will likely always be trouble. Every time they ask a question, they are pulling in someone else's time and thereby doubling the overall inactivity by taking up their own time and someone else's. It is important to remember that if you permit such poor behaviour, you are effectively promoting it.

Another personality type is the 'stepping stone'. This is an individual who is using your company as a stepping stone to bigger things further on. They appear to have a voracious appetite for work, they are bright, great with your clients, great with your team and they are just altogether fantastic. But, be aware that it's highly unlikely you will keep them for long. Wouldn't it be great if your whole team was filled with these people, endlessly ambitious, growing higher and higher and higher?. Unless your company can achieve a rapid rate of growth, these individuals will almost certainly outgrow your organisation within two to three years. My advice is - don't fear this. You will get a lot out of them during that time and they will also help other members of your staff. It is always a temptation to think that they are irreplaceable, but in my view no-one is ever irreplaceable. All you can do is wish these people well, keep in touch with them and hold them up as an example to others. In conclusion, therefore, there is nothing wrong with your company being seen as a stepping stone to other things. Who would you rather have working for you, ambitious types or languid dullards?

Feedback – Negative and Positive

Positive feedback is not part of a review but is the short message delivered ad hoc (I always think email is better for this because it's a permanent record). I think sparingly is best. In contrast, I believe negative feedback should be delivered in a much more extended and detailed way. The negative feedback should first of all outline what the problem is, as you see it, and then go on to provide the solution. Just remember that human beings will require five pieces of positive feedback for every one piece of negative feedback. There is a helpful acronym 'www.ebi' which stands for 'what's working well, even better if'. So in other words the employee you are giving negative feedback to is also told (at the same time) what they are doing right.

In British culture, we typically like to lay out negative feedback in the form of 'helpful advice', i.e. like it's a kind of tip for future success. Other cultures are much more direct and will just simply point out something that is wrong and how it should be corrected. Always make sure that if you are handing out negative feedback, the person that you are addressing it to has the opportunity to come and talk to you if they are unsure about what you are saying.

When it comes to giving praise, it is often easy to overlook the person who is a consistently high performer. It feels a little daft to be telling a person every single day "Oh that was great, that was great, and that was great". It sounds like you are overdoing it and that person will soon get bored with being told the same thing over and over again. However, it is important that these people are recognised regularly and that you don't take their performance for granted. If you are not careful, you can find that it is always the poor performers who get the congratulations when they do something right whereas the consistently good performers are ignored.

Dealing with Negative Nigels

These are the people for whom the glass is always half empty. For these people there is no solution that cannot be matched with an even bigger problem. Asking them to cheer up is about as useful as asking the rain to stop! My view on such people is that their personality is something you cannot change. Of course, there may be other factors in play here that cannot and should not be discounted, such as personal difficulties and mental health. So, with all things considered, the key thing is – do they perform? If they have a constantly negative attitude but are still performing very well, my suggestion is that they are the sort of person that can be a valuable asset to your team. The fact that they will always see the negatives in everything can, of itself, be very useful. They are like 'pit canaries' in that they will sound the alarm before anyone else realises the danger. In other words, the fact that they are negative is a possible asset to your team provided they are not disruptively negative. As ever, the key thing is always performance.

Creating the Right Climate

How do you create a climate? Wouldn't it be great if the sun shone every day? To your staff, to an extent, you **are** the weather system. If you come into the office in a bad mood, that bad mood will spread. If you are of a sunny and positive disposition, that will also spread. Everyone knows what the ideal climate should be and that is one where people are, generally speaking, positive about solving problems, they can collaborate freely with their immediate superior, and their views will be respected but challenged. They always know where to go for help and more importantly, they know what the overall objective of the company is. Employees that work for a boss who puts his/her own lifestyle requirements ahead of the customer's needs, despite the fact that he/she goes on and on about looking after the customer, will very soon lose respect from his/her team. Creating the right climate means empowering your staff to make decisions and take them away from you. If all the decisions require your sign off, very soon you will be overwhelmed. This is, of course, extremely difficult but if you get it right you will develop the right climate.

Resolving Conflict between Colleagues

If your colleague is a fellow football player in a team that is losing to its closest rivals, a raised voice on the field of play can be useful and instructive! In an office environment, however, I would suggest that there is no need whatsoever for a raised voice, unless there is an actual risk of physical danger, e.g. a fire. Anyone who raises their voice in an office environment is behaving inappropriately. The reality is that as human beings, we react negatively to such explosions and we get an adrenalin rush when faced with someone who has raised their voice against us. This is therefore not an environment that is going to be conducive to calm and rational decision making. Of course, it is important to have passion in your work but a passionate employee who raises their voice against another colleague is someone adding negativity to an office environment.

When two colleagues frequently bicker and argue, as the CEO you will need to step in. I have been in a situation where there was an extremely combative individual who released their anger and unpleasantness against two other colleagues in the office. It was not, however, that common and it was never in my presence. This led to me having complaints from the victims, but with me having not witnessed the event, who was I to believe? What I did in this instance was talk to other people in the office who were present whilst this went on and it wasn't long before I realised what the truth was. I had a meeting with the individual concerned and told her that her behaviour was unacceptable and if she did it one more time, she would get a written warning and a further outburst would lead to her dismissal. All was quiet for a little while until she could not contain herself any longer and duly lost the plot but, again, when I wasn't in the office. I issued the written warning, calm for a while and yet again it happened. Inevitably, she had to go. She too realised that she had to go. There are some people in this world who just cannot contain their emotions. They may be the most brilliant and talented people in the world, but you really don't need that level of disruption.

Employee conflict is not the same as employee debate. I have seen two employees arguing a point with some passion but never ever losing their temper with each other and discussing the point at length to try and achieve a solution. I have watched these discussions unfold in front of me, as if I wasn't there. Nothing pleases me more than to see my own employees talking things through at length, with enthusiasm and passion but crucially - without any negative emotion.

Building a High Performance Team...

...is a hard thing to do indeed! But it can be done and I have discovered over the years that there are pitfalls to avoid and opportunities to grasp. Firstly, be aware that age, gender and race are all irrelevant when building your team. It is easy to fall into the trap of thinking that you want people like you to build this great team. People who think the way you do, act the way you do, talk the way you do. The reality is that you need a diversity of ages, sexes and races. From that diversity will come a different way of looking at problems.

Although you would like your staff to be passionate about their views, a collaborative approach is always going to be more conducive to harmony and, crucially, to gaining positive results instead of a competitive culture. As human beings, we are naturally competitive, but it is better for your staff to reserve that competitive side of their behaviour for the firm as a whole rather than their position within the firm. If you can combine all of those competitive spirits into a common purpose of 'putting your clients' needs first' then a great team ethos can be developed. If everybody in the team believes that they are all going in the same direction and have the same purpose, there is a synergistic result.

In a positive team environment, everybody on the team has an opportunity to express their opinions. It is a temptation to just listen to the well spoken positive types but as previously mentioned in this book, the quietly or rarely spoken individuals need to be listened to as quite often their insight can be invaluable. There will always be somebody on the team who wants to hog the limelight by talking over their colleagues and generally being too loud. Their natural effervescence is, of course, useful but you can dial down their behaviour by giving a little bit more prominence to the quietly spoken individuals.

Working with people from different cultures means giving people space to celebrate their own culture. One obvious example of this is with religious festivities. Be sure that you recognise an individual's right to celebrate their own religious days and also remember that for some you will need to recognise their right to pray. Wherever possible, you should also provide space for this. Teams work better when all members of the team are seen to be treated equally and with respect.

Managing Employees' Reaction to Change

Much as some of us would like to think otherwise, change is constant. The phrase 'if it ain't broke, why fix it?' assumes the world never changes. That is simply not the case. In reality, constant change means there is a need for constant adapting. Some people relish a change and see it as an opportunity whilst other people may fear it. Your job as leader is to ensure that your staff can cope with any changes that will inevitably come over time. As the team leader, it is no good just telling your people "things are going to change and this is what's going to happen". You need to sell to them the reasons behind the change. This means telling people what the consequences are of not changing, and what opportunities the change will present to everybody. This selling process, because that is what it is, should be undertaken some time in advance of the change taking place. My preference is to do it in writing and give members of staff time to come and see you individually to talk through the impact. What everybody wants to know, of course, is what's in it for them, what are the consequences for them, what are the new opportunities that would be presented by the change.

One of the key aspects in the communication of potential change is that you must be clear that there is no alternative. If there is resistance from any particular members of staff, those members of staff must be told that the direction of the company is now set, and if that is not in the direction in which they want to go in, they must make their decisions accordingly. If the implementation of the change is planned sufficiently in advance, those who don't want to go along with it will have time to make alternative plans.

The follow up to the change is for you to repeat the plan and the implementation of the plan at staff meetings. The reality is that people will forget what they have been told, and they will need to be reminded on a frequent basis. Furthermore, staff meetings will enable these matters to be discussed openly and the staff are able to put you on the spot for you to answer all their questions.

One of the key objections to change is often lack of resources. People will say "how can we do such and such, we haven't got the necessary IT or software to make that happen". It is always better to anticipate those objections in advance and to be able to provide the answers. You will need to know where the IT and software is going to come from and where extra resources are going to be found.

Communicate, communicate, communicate. When it comes to management change there is no substitute for frequent communication. That communication should always be delivered in a positive way. It is inevitable that some members of staff will be more enthusiastic about the possibilities than others. If it is possible to appoint people who can assist in implementing the change, then clearly the ones you should be selecting are the enthusiastic ones. They are also in a position to help you sell the idea of the changes to the more reluctant staff.

Managing Creativity within the Team

If you think that you, as the owner and leader of this company, know everything then you are wrong! Hopefully your team will be made up of young people, old people and people from different ethnicities. They will have a different way of viewing the challenges that you face, and will therefore have different solutions, particularly if they are younger and more knowledgeable around the technology than you are.

The key thing is to be open to new ideas at all times. If you give the impression that you don't want to change your ways or that the way things are is just fine, then your team will very quickly stop feeding you new ideas. New ideas should ideally come to you in the form of a verbal discussion initially, to be followed up by the proposal in writing. Any proposal should be brief. The next stage is for you to think about that carefully but you must ensure that you have a full discussion with the individual who has made the suggestion and if you genuinely think it is not going to work, you need to tell them why. But be sure to encourage them, offer your gratitude and suggest some potential alternatives. Maybe suggest that they go away and think about it, or talk to some other members of the team and come up with a plan that is different and even better in a number of ways that you will then describe.

If you have ambitious people working for you they will have a constant flow of ideas and you would be a fool to ignore that treasure trove coming your way!

THE END

LET THEM MANAGE was written to put the responsibility **back** on business owners to look after the people working for them and to have an understanding of how their teams are being built. This does not negate the need to have a suitable HR function if your organisation was large enough, but those departments should only be used when it is relevant to do so.

There are times when you will find the resources of energy and time will prevent your involvement, but it does not remove your **responsibility**.

If you are looking for assistance in managing your personnel and making sure all the legalities are accounted for, please don't hesitate to get in touch. Otherwise, all there is to say is "I'll let **you** manage".

Robert Stell
Robert@bradburystell.co.uk

Appendix I
CONTRACT OF EMPLOYMENT

_____(name of the business)

Introduction

Section 1 of the Employment Rights Act 2008 requires certain basic terms of employment to be notified to all employees within two months of the employee commencing work. This document complies with that requirement.

From: _____ (name of the business) ('we' 'us' 'our' or 'the Company') of

_____(address)

To: _____ of _____

_____ (address) ('you' 'your').

1. General

1.1   The following particulars are given to you in accordance with the terms of the Employment Rights Act 2008 and other relevant legislation.

1.2   In accepting your appointment it shall be deemed that you have accepted all the terms and conditions set out in this document.

1.3   Any earlier offer or agreement made in respect of your employment with the Company which contradicts or conflicts with anything in this document is null and void and superseded by this document.

2. Continuous Employment

2.1   Your period of continuous employment with us began on the _____ of _____ _____ .

2.2   No employment with a previous employer counts as part of your period of continuous employment.

3. Probationary Period

The first ____ months of your employment will be a probationary period. During this period your performance and conduct will be monitored. At the end of the probationary period your appointment may be confirmed or your probationary period extended.

4. Place of work

4.1   Your normal place of work will be at _____.

4.2   The Company may change your place of work and/or may require you to work at other locations within a reasonable distance of your current place of work either on a temporary or permanent basis.

5. Reporting

You will be reporting to _____, whose job title is _____. Other managers may also act as your line manager.

6. Collective agreements

There are no collective agreements relevant to your employment.

7. Job title

7.1 You are employed as a _____.

7.2 It may be necessary in the interests of the Company as a whole for changes to be made to your job title or your job description. Within reason, your existing duties may be changed and/or new duties may be added or taken away. Any significant changes will only be made after due consultation with you.

8. Pay

8.1 You will be paid _____ by cheque or credit transfer to your bank account in arrears at the rate of £_____ gross each month (and proportionately for any lesser period, each pay instalment being deemed to accrue rateably from day to day).

8.2 Overtime is not paid unless the period of overtime, and the hourly rate of overtime pay, has been agreed and authorised in writing by your line manager before you work the overtime.

9. Hours of work

9.1 Your normal working hours are _____ am to _____ pm, Mondays to Fridays.

9.2 Your lunch break is _____ minutes. Your lunch break is not working time and is not paid.

9.3 You are allowed to take tea breaks of ____ minutes each morning and ____ minutes each afternoon. Tea breaks are counted as working time and are paid.

9.4 In certain circumstances it may be necessary to change, reduce or increase your normal working hours to ensure that your duties are properly performed.

9.5 From time to time, you may be requested to work overtime, paid or unpaid, and you will be expected to co-operate with any reasonable request. Overtime will be paid only if the period of overtime and the hourly rate of overtime pay, has been agreed and authorised in writing by your line manager, or a member of senior management, before you work the overtime.

10. Sickness absence

10.1   You are required to contact your line manager or a senior member of management by your normal start time on the first day of sickness absence, stating why you are absent and when you expect to return. If your absence continues, you must contact the Company regularly to update on your continuing absence.

10.2   You must provide the appropriate certificates at the relevant times, and complete any absence recording documentation as required on your return to work. If you are unclear as to the appropriate certificates please ask your line manager.

10.3   Please note that personal contact is required at all times when contacting the Company. The sending of text messages will not be accepted as notification.

10.4   Failure to notify the Company as set out may result in the Disciplinary Procedure being used.

10.5   You should produce the following written evidence of absence and ensure that appropriate certificates are provided for the whole of your absence: (a) Self-Certificate for absence of up to and including seven calendar days; or (b) Medical Practitioner's Certificate (known as a 'Fit Note') for absence of more than seven calendar days.

10.6   You should forward certificates and any correspondence to the Company as soon as possible. Failure to do so may result in sick pay being delayed or withheld and disciplinary action being taken.

10.7   The Company reserves the right to require you to undertake a medical examination by a medical practitioner and/or specialist of the Company's choice and/or to seek a report from your doctor (subject to your rights under the Access to Medical Reports Act 1998).

10.8   For the purposes of the Statutory Sick Pay scheme the agreed 'qualifying days' are Monday to Friday.

10.9   There is no right to contractual sick pay but such payments may be made at the discretion of the Company.

10.10 A Fit Note is not conclusive evidence that an employee is unfit to work and the Company reserves the right to make appropriate enquires to ascertain whether an employee is fit enough to do different or lighter duties.

11. Holidays

11.1 The holiday year runs from the ___ of _____ to the ___ of _____ each year.

11.2 Your holiday entitlement will be the statutory holiday entitlement. This is currently 28 days each holiday year if you work 5 days a week.

11.3 If you work part-time, your holiday entitlement is calculated according to the number of days/hours you work in proportion to the Company's normal working week.

11.4 The following eight Bank/Public Holidays are included in your holiday entitlement: New Years Day, Good Friday, Easter Monday, May Day Bank Holiday, Monday Spring Bank Holiday, Monday Late Summer Bank Holiday, Christmas Day and Boxing Day.

11.5 Payment for holidays will be at your normal rate of pay.

11.6 Untaken holiday in a holiday year cannot be carried over to the next holiday year except with the permission of your line manager or another senior member of management.

11.7 The preceding sub-paragraph does not apply to women on maternity leave, fathers on extended paternity leave or those who are or have been on sick leave where holidays have accrued. Such employees are entitled by law to carry over untaken holiday into the next holiday year.

12. Pension

The Company does not operate a pension scheme applicable to your employment but will facilitate your access to a designated stakeholder pension scheme to the extent it is obliged to do so as a matter of law.

13. Termination of employment

13.1 The notice required by either of us to terminate your employment will be the statutory notice which is: one week's notice if you have been continuously employed for up to two years; and then one week's notice for each completed year of employment from two completed years up to a maximum of twelve weeks' notice.

13.2 We reserve the right in our absolute discretion to pay you basic salary in lieu of notice.

14. Lay offs and short-time working

14.1 Although every reasonable effort will always be made to ensure full employment, in the event of a temporary shortage of work, the Company reserves the right to temporarily layoff or place on shorttime working any employees affected.

14.2 If you are laid off or are placed on short working you will have certain statutory rights in connection with the lay-off. Please ask your line manager for more information.

15. Changes to this document

The Company reserves the right, after due consultation with you, to change your terms and conditions of employment if the changes are necessary and reasonable for a business or any other substantial reason. Any significant change(s) will be confirmed in writing within four weeks of the change(s).

16. Contract of Employment

By signing below you confirm that you accept this document as your contract of employment.

Signed _____ (employee)

Dated _____ of _____ 202..

Signed _____ (for employer)

Dated _____ of _____ 202..

Appendix II
DIRECTOR SERVICE AGREEMENT

THIS DIRECTOR SERVICE AGREEMENT (the "Agreement"), which includes particulars pursuant to the Employment Rights Act 1996, is entered into upon the XXX day of XXX;

BETWEEN:

1.   XXX, a Private Limited Company located at XXX (the "Company"); and

2.   XXX of XXX (the "Director" or "you").

IT IS HEREBY AGREED as follows:

1.   Definitions and Interpretation

1.   In this Agreement, except to the extent that the context otherwise requires, the following terms shall have the meanings set forth below:

"Board" means the directors for the time being of the Company;

"Business" means all activities and functions of the Company, both internally and external-facing;

"Business Day" means a day (other than a Saturday or Sunday) on which banks are generally open in England for the transaction of normal banking business;

"Design" means any design which is registrable under the Registered Designs Act 1949 or in respect of which design rights subsist under section 213 of the Copyright, Designs and Patents Act 1988;

"Drawing" means any drawing, picture, photograph, plan or sketch in any form;

"Invention" means any invention whether patentable or not under the Patents Act 1977 or by virtue of any international convention or treaty, together with the right to apply in any part of the world for appropriate protection therefor;

"Know-how" means any method, technique, discovery, secret process or the like not amounting to an Invention, and any associated data or technical information;

"Records" means any samples, models, documents (as defined in section 13 of the Civil Evidence Act 1995), notebooks or other records in any form, including data stored in a computer or otherwise; and

"Software" means any computer programs, web or mobile applications, including preparatory design material therefor, any documentation relating thereto, and any media containing or recording any part of any of the foregoing items.

1.2 In this Agreement, unless the context otherwise requires:

(a) words importing the singular include the plural and vice versa, words importing a gender include every gender;

(b) any reference to a statutory provision shall include such provision and any regulations made in pursuance thereof as from time to time modified or re-enacted;

(c) headings are for convenience of reference only and shall not affect the interpretation of this Agreement.

2. Appointment

2.1 You shall be an employee of the company with the job title of XXX. You agree to undertake other duties as may from time to time be reasonably required.

3. Place of Work

3.1 Your primary location or work shall be XXX.

3.2 You accept that you will work at any other establishment of the Company within the United Kingdom whether on a temporary or permanent basis as your contract with the Company shall so require for the needs of the Business. You also agree that you will make visits to clients or partners of the Company throughout the United Kingdom and abroad as may be required from time to time.

4. Duration

4.1 Your employment with the Company under this Agreement commences on XXX and shall continue indefinitely until terminated in accordance with clause 19 below.

4.2 The first XXX months are a probationary period, at the end of which your employment may be terminated immediately without reason. The Company reserves the right to extend this probationary period by up to a further XXX months.

5. Outside Interests

5.1 You shall not undertake work outside of the Company that may amount to a conflict of interest with the Company, and you shall not have any interest, whether directly or indirectly, in a business that may place you in a conflict of interest with the Company. You shall not undertake work outside of the Company which, in the reasonable opinion of the

Board, may interfere with the proper performance of your duties in the Company.

5.2 Notwithstanding clause 5.1, you shall be permitted to hold up to a maximum of XXX percent of the issued shares or other securities of any class of any company whatsoever which is listed or traded on a recognised stock exchange.

6. Salary and Payments

6.1 Your basic rate of pay is £ XXX per year, payable XXX in arrears on the XXX, which is inclusive of any fees to which you shall be entitled as a director of the Company.

6.2 Overtime shall not be payable.

6.3 All pay shall be subject to statutory deductions including but not limited to PAYE and National Insurance.

6.4 All payments shall be made directly to your nominated bank or building society account.

6.5 If any loan, advance, or erroneous payment is made to you by the Company, the Company reserves the right to demand immediate repayment or deduct such amounts from any future payments made to you.

7. Expenses

7.1 Out of pocket expenses incurred by you solely in connection with the Business will be reimbursed promptly upon the presentation of a duly completed approved expense form along with the supporting receipts, provided that prior permission to incur such expenses has been obtained from the Board.

8. Hours of Work

8.1 The Company's normal hours of work are XXX which may be amended from time to time.

8.2 You shall be entitled to take a lunch break of one hour during each working day. Your lunch break does not form part of your working hours.

8.3 The Company reserves the right to require you to work additional or alternate hours from time to time as may reasonably be required for the proper performance of your duties and this has been taken into consideration in determining your pay and conditions of employment. For the avoidance of doubt, you shall not be required to work in excess of the working week as set out in the Working Time Regulations 1998, unless agreed in writing that this limit should not apply.

8.4 You shall arrive to work on time as consistent with the normal hours of work or as otherwise instructed.

9. Duties

9.1 You shall faithfully and diligently perform such duties and job functions in accordance with your role as a Director, and in the capacity specified in clause 2.1, as may be required or instructed and you shall at all times use your best endeavours to further the Business.

9.2 You shall observe and comply with all lawful and proper orders and directions which may be given to you in connection with your employment and with any statutory requirements or other regulations for the time being in force.

9.3 You shall observe and obey the Company's established policies and procedures, which shall be made available to you upon request. The Company may make updates to the policies and procedures from time to time.

9.4 You shall not at any time do anything, or omit to do anything, which may in the reasonable opinion of the Board bring the Company into disrepute or harm the goodwill or the reputation of the Company.

10. Holiday

10.1 The holiday year runs from XXX to XXX.

10.2 Your entitlement to paid holiday in a holiday year is based on the number of complete months you have worked in that year. Holiday accrues at the rate of one-twelfth of your annual entitlement for each complete calendar month of service during the holiday year.

10.3 Your entitlement to paid holiday is XXX in each complete holiday year, inclusive of all UK statutory and bank holidays. Authorised holiday absences within your entitlement will be paid at your basic rate of pay.

10.4 Holiday dates must be authorised by the Board in advance, which reserves the right to refuse any dates which are inconvenient to the Business or clash with the holidays of other members of the Board. You should not purchase tickets or commit to other holiday related expenditure before you have obtained the necessary authorisation for your choice of dates.

10.5 The Company reserves the right to require you to take certain days as part of your paid annual holiday entitlement, whether for an annual shutdown, customary holidays, to comply with Working Time Regulations, or arising from the needs of the Business.

10.6 Unless specifically directed otherwise by the Board, you are required to take a day of your annual leave entitlement on every bank/public holiday that falls on a day when you would normally be at work, as part of your paid annual holiday entitlement.

10.7 If you do not take all the holiday you are entitled to in a holiday year, then you shall not be entitled to carry forward your entitlement unless you fulfil specific legal exemption criteria for this rule. Unused holidays may not be enchashed.

10.8 Following the termination of your employment, your final pay shall be adjusted accordingly up or down for unused or excess holiday entitlement, one day of holiday being worth 1/260th of your basic annual salary, except for:

(a) if you are dismissed for gross misconduct, or leave without giving or working proper notice, in which case you shall be entitled to accrued holiday pay of no more than £25; or

(b) if the adjusted amount for excess holiday taken is more than your final pay, in which case you shall owe such balance to the Company, payable upon your last day of work.

11. Health and Safety

11.1 You shall take reasonable care for the health and safety of yourself and other persons who may be affected by your acts or omissions at work. As regards to any duty or requirements imposed on the Company under any health and safety legislation, you shall co-operate with the Company so far as necessary to enable such duty or requirement to be conformed or complied with.

12. Absence and Sickness

12.1 If you shall at any time be unable to work as a result of illness, injury, accident or any other circumstances beyond your control, you shall for the first XXX weeks of your inability to work in any XXX month period be entitled to receive your normal basic rate of pay, minus any applicable statutory sick pay claimed, and thereafter only at the sole and absolute discretion of the Board.

12.2 If you are unable to work you shall inform a member of the Board by telephone at the start of the first day of such absence. In the event that your inability to work persists for longer than XXX consecutive Business Days, you shall present to the board upon request documentary evidence of the causal illness, injury or accident.

12.3 It is expected that employees who are absent because of sickness will act in such manner to facilitate their return to work as soon as possible whilst at the same time the Company recognises the need for employees to be fit and well and would not expect an employee to return before fully recovered. The fact that an employee is unable to work means that, normally, the employee would not be expected to take part in other activities. To that end, you shall not:

(a)   take part in any sports, hobbies or social activities which are inconsistent with your illness and are not for recuperative purposes. In particular, activities which could prolong or aggravate any injury or could delay recovery should not be carried out; or

(b)   carry out any other employment or work, whether it is paid or unpaid; or

(c)   engage in any activity that is inconsistent with the nature of your illness (for example shopping if you allege that you are bedridden).

12.4   You should not return to work until you have been certified as fit to return to work in cases where a premature return to work may affect your physical or mental well-being or create a risk to health and safety.

12.5   Whenever possible, appointments for visiting the doctor, dentist, hospital or similar should be made outside of normal work hours.

12.6   Maternity, paternity, adoption, parental, and dependant's leave shall be provided in line with the statutory provisions. You are requested to inform the Board as soon as practicable if you anticipate the need to exercise such statutory rights.

12.7   If you are called for Jury Service or court proceedings, you must notify you're the Board as soon as possible. You may be required to present the Jury Service Notification Slip or the Court Slip. Unpaid leave of absence shall be granted and you are expected to return to work when adjournment makes return practicable.

13.   Medical Examinations

13.1   In the event of reasonable concern about your health, and the ability to carry out your work, the Board reserves the right to ask you to submit to a medical examination at any time, the cost of which will be borne by the Company and carried out by a doctor of the Company's choice. The Board will adhere to all statutory requirements in making such a request.

14.   Ethics

14.1   You shall attempt to avoid any situation in which there is a conflict between your personal interests and the Company's interests, and if such a situation arises you shall discuss it with the Board at the earliest reasonable opportunity.

14.2   You shall not use your authority or position in employment for any secret or improper personal gain whether for yourself or others.

14.3   In relation to any function of a public nature, any activity connected with the Business, or any activity performed in the course of your employment, you must not:

(a) directly or indirectly, offer, promise or give a financial or other advantage to another person:

(i) attempting to induce that person or another to perform improperly a function or activity, or

(ii) to reward that person or another for performing improperly a function or activity; or

(b) directly or indirectly, request, agree to receive, or accept a financial or other advantage (whether for yourself or another person) as an incentive to the improper performance of any function or activity; or

(c) in anticipation or in consequence of your requesting, agreeing to receive or accepting a financial or other advantage:

(i) perform or request that another person perform a function or activity improperly, or

(ii) assent or acquiesce in the improper performance by another person of a function or activity.

15. Confidentiality

15.1 Except as otherwise specifically required for the duties of your employment, you agree to keep strictly secret and confidential, and under no circumstances to disclose to any third party, any sensitive or confidential information, or trade secrets, disclosed to you in connection with the Business or your employment.

15.2 Notwithstanding Clause 15.1, the confidentiality obligation shall not apply to:

(a) any information disclosed to you which becomes generally known to the public, other than by reason of your own wilful or negligent act or omission;

(b) any information which is required to be disclosed pursuant to any applicable laws or to any competent governmental or statutory authority or pursuant to rules or regulations of any relevant regulatory, administrative or supervisory body; or

(c) any information disclosed confidentially to your own professional legal or financial adviser.

15.3 The obligations set out in this clause 15 shall survive the termination of this Agreement.

16. Intellectual Property

16.1 Any Invention or Know-how which is made, obtained, acquired, produced or found by you during the course of your employment shall, subject to the provisions of the Patents Act 1977, belong exclusively to the

Company, and you shall upon making, obtaining, acquiring, producing or finding such Invention or Know-how forthwith disclose the same to the Company or as it may direct.

16.2 You and the Company each shall keep confidential any Invention that you disclose to the Company until its ownership has been determined. If the Invention is determined by a competent authority to belong to you, the Company shall thereafter continue to keep it confidential, but shall have XXX days from the date of its disclosure to the Company to consider whether to make an offer for it, during which time you shall not disclose, license or assign the Invention to any other person or entity. If the Invention is determined by a competent authority to belong to the Company, you shall thereafter continue to keep it confidential in accordance with clause 15.

16.3 Your signature of assent as inventor, which may be required for, or which forms part of, any application for protection of any Invention which belongs to or is acquired by the Company, shall operate as a your binding acknowledgement that, insofar as the subject of that application is not already vested in the Company by operation of law, it is one in respect of which the right to apply for protection, the right to claim priority for that application under any treaty, convention or otherwise and the beneficial interest in any protection that may be obtained, is vested in the Company.

16.4 All Designs, Drawings, Records and Software which are made by you in the course of your employment shall belong exclusively to the Company, together with any copyright or design therein, whether registrable or unregistrable, the right to apply throughout the world for appropriate protection therefor, whether by virtue of any treaty, convention or otherwise, and all other rights of a like nature therein which are conferred under the laws of the United Kingdom and all other countries of the world, for the full term thereof and any renewals or extensions thereof.

16.5 In respect of any Invention made by you which belongs to or is acquired by the Company and any Design made by you in the course of your employment, you shall, if and when required to do so by the Company, at any time both during the period or after the termination of your employment, and at the Company's expense but for no further consideration:

(a) furnish any description, drawing, specification or other information which the Company may require in relation to such Invention or Design;

(b) apply for or join in applying for a patent, registered design or such other protection as the Company may require in relation to such Invention or Design; and

(c) execute all such documents and do all such acts and things as the

Company may reasonably require to obtain such patent, registered design or other protection and to vest the same and all rights therein and the title thereto absolutely in the Company or in such persons as the Company may direct and to maintain such patent, registered design or other protection in force or to extend the term thereof.

16.6 At any time during your employment upon request by the Board or upon the termination of your employment, you shall forthwith deliver up to the Company all Designs, Drawings, Records and Software which are made by you in the course of your employment.

16.7 The obligations set out in this clause 16 shall survive the termination of this Agreement.

17. Staff Records

17.1 You agree to allow the Company, for the duration of your employment and for a period of up to XXX months thereafter, to create, store, alter or retrieve personal data about you in connection with your employment, including but not limited to that which relates to your computer activities, performance, health, attendance, education, prior employment and experience, and interests.

17.2 You agree to provide contact details to the Company including your address and telephone number, and those of a next of kin, and you shall update the Company immediately upon any changes thereof.

17.3 You shall be entitled upon request to access any information held about you by the Company, subject to the Data Protection Act.

18. Security and Property

18.1 You hereby acknowledge that the Company's computer and communications systems are critical to the Business. You shall not do anything, or omit to do anything, which leads to or might reasonably be believed to lead to a compromise of the Company's computer or communications systems. You shall:

(a) not disclose, or permit to be disclosed, your password to anyone at any time;

(b) access and make alterations only in such parts of the computer system which are necessary for you to carry out your normal duties, or such other parts for which you have been specifically authorised and then only as needed in relation to that specific situation;

(c) not under any circumstances install any computer software onto any computer system unless it has been virus-checked and expressly authorised by the Board;

(d) use the email and internet facilities only in connection with the Business, or otherwise in such a manner as not to interfere with the performance of your employment;

(e)   not send any communication containing language or content that might be considered as offensive, obscene or derogatory, defamatory, encouraging criminal purposes, or damaging to any person or the Company's image or reputation;

(f)   not use any computer or communications system in connection with any unlawful purpose, or infringe upon any intellectual property rights or copyright; and

(g)   at all times use the computer and communications systems only with highest degree of care, respect and professionalism.

18.2   In the event that you are given keys or access materials for the Company's premises or equipment, you shall not allow, or permit to be allowed, copies to be made or any other person to use such keys or access materials without the express permission of the Board. You shall return such keys or access materials immediately upon the Board's request.

18.3   You shall not leave any of your valuable personal items unattended on the Company's premises. The Company takes no responsibility for loss, damage or theft of any personal property.

19.   Notice and Termination

19.1   In the event of gross misconduct the Company may terminate this Agreement without prior notice or payment in lieu thereof.

19.2   Other than in the event of gross misconduct, this Agreement may be terminated with the serving to the other party of the following period of notice:

(a)   by the Company, no notice during the first one month of employment, thereafter one week during the first two complete years' service, and thereafter one week for each complete year of service up to a maximum of twelve weeks; or

(b)   by you, one week.

[note that the above notice periods in section (a) are the statutory minimums. they may be altered in favour of the employee]

19.3   You and the Company agree that any notice pursuant to clause 19.2 shall be made in writing.

19.4   During your notice period, whether notice has been given by you or by the Company, the Company may:

(a)   require you to take any outstanding accrued holiday entitlement;

(b) require that you do not take holiday booked in your notice period even if such holiday had previously been authorised, but work out your complete period of notice;

(c) assign different duties to you, which may be of a lesser scope than you were previously carrying out; or

(d) require you not to attend your normal place of work, but to remain at home during normal working hours, in which event and for such period, any express or implied term requiring the Company to provide you with work is expressly excluded, and you must be available for meetings or telephone conferences during working hours as required.

19.5 In the event that you fail to provide or work out proper notice, you shall forfeit any right to accrued holiday pay and other contractual payments except to the extent that such payments are required by law.

19.6 Upon termination of your employment for whatever reason, you shall:

(a) immediately return all Company property in your possession including without limitation data, confidential information or any other intellectual property, mobile communications or computer equipment, keys or access materials, or any other physical property, and you agree not to make or retain copies of any Company property;

(b) execute and do and take all such steps as may be necessary, including fully co-operating with the Board, to facilitate your removal from the Company to the fullest extent possible, including without limitation the filing of your resignation as a Director with the relevant statutory bodies and the removal of yourself as a signatory of any and all bank accounts belonging to the Company; and

(c) not at any time thereafter represent yourself as being in any way employed, connected with or having an interest in the Company.

19.7 The Company reserves the right to suspend you on full basic pay at the Company's sole and absolute discretion. Suspension may be imposed to assist in orderly investigations of potential grievance or disciplinary matters, to allow a cooling-off period, or in other necessary circumstances. Suspension shall not be regarded as a disciplinary penalty, and shall carry no implication of guilt. While on suspension, you must be available for work or meetings if required during your normal working hours. In the event of dismissal for gross misconduct, you shall have no right to pay for any period of suspension immediately preceding such dismissal.

20. Restrictions

20.1 For a period of XXX months following the termination of your employment for whatever reason, you shall not:

(a) solicit or attempt to solicit business from any person or entity who shall have been a client or customer or potential customer of the Company during the XXX months preceding such termination;

(b) persuade or attempt to persuade any person to leave the employment of the Company or to cease to provide services to the Company; or

(c) employ or attempt to employ the services of any person who was an employee or consultant of the Company during the XXX months preceding such termination.

21. Pension

21.1 You hereby give the Employer an opt-in notice requesting to join the Employer's pension scheme in accordance with section 7 of the Pensions Act 2008, subject to the Employer's legal obligations and/or any specific legal exemptions under the Pensions Act 2008.

21.2 Upon the Employer enrolling you into the Employer's pension scheme, the Employer shall notify you in writing of the date of enrolment, the pension scheme type and its provider, the contributions of you and the Employer, and your right to opt out.

22. Miscellaneous

22.1 During normal working hours, including break times, you shall refrain from taking part in recreational activities that could result in damage to property or personal injury.

22.2 You shall at all times refrain from smoking on the Company's premises.

22.3 There are no collective agreements in force which affect the terms of your employment.

22.4 The failure of the Company to exercise or enforce any right conferred upon it by this Agreement shall not be deemed to be a waiver of any such right or operate so as to bar the exercise or enforcement thereof at any time(s) thereafter, as a waiver of another or constitute a continuing waiver.

22.5 No exercise of discretion by the Company whatsoever shall give rise to any future rights of the Director or obligations of the Company.

22.6 Without prejudice to any rights in respect of actions relating to fraudulent misrepresentation, this Agreement and any documents referred to herein constitute the entire understanding between you and the Company with respect to the subject matter thereof and supersedes all prior agreements, negotiations and discussions between you and the Company relating thereto.

22.7 The unenforceability of any single provision of this Agreement shall not affect any other provision hereof.

22.8 This Agreement shall be governed by and construed in accordance with English law, and you and the Company each irrevocably submit to the exclusive jurisdiction of the English courts over any claim, dispute or matter arising under or in connection with this Agreement or its enforceability.

IN WITNESS WHEREOF this Agreement has been executed as of the day first above written.

Company Director

Signed _____

Name _____

Title _____

Date _____